When God Converts a Sinner

When God Converts a Sinner

Confessional Perspectives on
Justification and the Christian Life

Douglas Vickers

WIPF & STOCK · Eugene, Oregon

WHEN GOD CONVERTS A SINNER
Confessional Perspectives on Justification and the Christian Life

Wipf & Stock
A Division of Wipf and Stock Publishers
199 W. 8th Ave., Suite 3
Eugene, OR 97401

www.wipfandstock.com

ISBN 13: 978-1-55635-982-8

Manufactured in the U.S.A.

Scripture quotations are from the King James Version.

Contents

Preface

THE TITLE I HAVE chosen is taken from the *Westminster Confession of Faith*, as will be explained more fully in chapter 5. The doctrinal theology that descended from the Reformation received its highest English language expression in the expansive literature of the seventeenth century and in the Confessions of Faith that were produced at that time, the *Westminster Confession of Faith* (1647), the *Savoy Declaration of Faith* (1658), and the *Second London (Baptist) Confession* (1689). My objective in this brief work is to confront a number of questions that arise from a consideration of four chapters that are common to those confessions: chapter 9, "Of Free Will," chapter 11, "Of Justification," chapter 12, "Of Adoption," and chapter 14, "Of Saving Faith."

In chapter 1 I indicate the principal questions that stand at the heart of Christian belief. Those questions have to do with the relation between God's existence outside of time and the entry into time of the Second Person of the Godhead for the accomplishment of redemption; the nature of saving faith and the freedom from the entailment of sin which, as a result of redemption, accrues to the Christian believer; the reality of the Christian believer's union with Christ; and some consequent aspects of the God-man relation in the Christian's life journey.

Contemporary theological discussion has clouded the meaning and import of the confessional statements I have referred to and has shunted the church away from its earlier and more secure moorings. There is reason to believe, as a result, that an elevation to prominence of what the earlier and classic confessions of faith have said might at this time contribute to a renewed and clearer understanding of the faith that the church at large is called to confess.

Chapter 3 began life as a paper delivered to the 2007 Annual Conference of the Reformed Congregational Fellowship (RCF), and chapters 5 through 7 first appeared as papers presented to the New England Reformed Fellowship (NERF) in 2006 and 2007. The papers are reproduced here with minimal editorial alteration. I am indebted to the organizing committees of RCF and NERF for their courtesies and to the lively discussions that followed the presentation of the papers.

The unity of the work is established by the sequential discussion of the issues raised in chapters 1 and 2. The chapters that follow align with the statements of relevant doctrines as they are addressed in the Confessions I have referred to. Chapter 7 presents a more direct critique of arguments contained in the literature of the New Perspective on Paul, the Federal Vision theology, Shepardism, and the separate attempts by Richard Gaffin and Michael Horton to effect a paradigm shift in Reformed theology.

My heavy indebtedness to a long line of Reformed theologians will be apparent to the informed reader. We stand on the shoulders of better scholars who have preceded us. I record happily that in the development of my own theology I owe a particular debt to the work of the twentieth-century theologian-apologist Cornelius Van Til. My work in books and research papers, during both my professorship in a non-theological discipline and my writing in doctrinal and apologetic theology in recent years, has had the very valuable editorial assistance of Ann Hopkins and I record my deepest thanks to her. I have benefited from the theological insights and pastoral ministry of Dr. Robert E. Davis of Millers Falls, Massachusetts, and I am deeply grateful for his encouragement in my work. Through what has been a long academic and publishing career my wife, Miriam, has given me support whose value cannot be measured or spoken by any words in this short space.

For whatever blemishes and infelicities remain in the work I take full responsibility.

The Issue Stated

IT IS CLEAR FROM a survey of the contemporary scene that we live in an age of theological innovation and doctrinal discount. Old established understandings of "the faith once delivered to the saints" (Jude 3) are under attack, disturbing the peace of the church, tarnishing its witness, and challenging its purity. Theology, it appears, has lost its earlier and secure moorings. New prophets peddle lesser preoccupations and arguments grounded in shallower presuppositions. Several questions, as a result, engage the reflective Christian mind.

First, given the mystery of the relation between eternity and time, what was involved in the incarnation in this world of the second Person of the Godhead who came as Jesus Christ to be our redeemer? For the gospel declares that "when the fulness of the time was come, God sent forth his Son, made of a woman, made under the law, to redeem them that were under the law, that we might receive the adoption of sons" (Gal. 4:4–5); that "God . . . loved us, and sent his Son to be the propitiation for our sins" (1 John 4:10); and that "in due time Christ died for the ungodly" (Rom. 5:6). Here we confront the reality that the Son of God came from his timeless eternity "in the bosom of the Father" (John 1:18) and entered into the time that he had created, in doing so making himself subject to time in order to accomplish salvation for his people. That salvation had been ordained before the foundation of the world and was now to be brought to effect.

Second, what is to be understood as the theological grounding of the statement of the confessions that "The grace of faith, whereby the elect are enabled to believe . . . is the work of the Spirit of Christ in their hearts"?[1] In what respects are the Persons of the Godhead jointly engaged

---

1. Westminster Confession, XIV, 1.

in the accomplishment and application to individuals of the benefits of redemption, and what relations do the identities of the redeemed bear to the divine decrees and intentions? In the context of redemption, what is to be understood as saving faith and the individual's capacity and ability to believe?

Third, in what sense is it true and meaningful for the Christian life that "If the Son therefore shall make you free, ye shall be free indeed" (John 8:36)? What is to be said, by way of implication, of the bondage of the human will in the state of sin to which Adam's dereliction from his covenantal obligations reduced us? And the question follows, is the gospel statement directed to a freedom of the will that the regenerating grace of God conveys to the Christian believer? The seventeenth-century confessions to which we shall return observe that "When God converts a sinner, and translates him into the state of grace, he freeth him from his natural bondage under sin."[2] But what, it needs to be asked, are the possibilities for Christian living that follow? What is implied in the apostolic injunction, "Stand fast therefore in the liberty wherewith Christ hath made us free, and be not entangled again with the yoke of bondage" (Gal. 5:1)?

Fourth, why, how, and with what results, do conditions arise in the Christian life in which the cry of the Psalmist becomes all too relevant, "Cast me not away from thy presence; and take not thy holy spirit from me. Restore unto me the joy of thy salvation; and uphold me with thy free spirit" (Ps. 51:11–12)? The confessions again observe that Christian believers "may by their sins fall under God's fatherly displeasure, and not have the light of his countenance restored unto them, until they humble themselves, confess their sins, beg pardon, and renew their faith and repentance."[3] What is to be said, in the light of that possibility, of the promise of our Lord that "I will pray the Father, and he shall give you another Comforter, that he may abide with you for ever; even the Spirit of truth . . . he dwelleth with you, and shall be in you" (John 14:16–17)? What is it, then, in which the believer's eternal security consists, and what guarantees his access to the eternal inheritance that has been promised him in Christ (Heb. 9:15)?

Fifth, in the light of the answers to these questions, what is to be said of the doctrinal and practical significance of the Christian believer's adoption into the family of God and, as a result, his or her indissoluble union

2. Westminster Confession, IX, 4.
3. Ibid., XI, 5.

with Christ? "Adoption," the Westminster Shorter Catechism declares, "is an act of God's free grace, whereby we are received into the number, and have a right to all the privileges of the sons of God."[4] And the apostle to the Gentiles states that the very meaning of salvation resides in the fact that "ye have received the Spirit of adoption, whereby we cry, Abba, Father" (Rom. 8:15). It will be seen at more length that the high privileges the Christian believer enjoys turn for their reality and significance on the imputation to him of the righteousness of Christ. For in the once-for-all declarative-forensic statement of God that establishes the sinner's justification, the believer's title to heaven and his prospect of eternal inheritance are secured. But if, as the Scriptures abundantly declare, that is so, what is to be said of certain contemporary claims that the imputation of the righteousness of Christ at the point of justification does not suffice? What is to be said by way of response to the claim that certain good works of the Christian contribute to one's final and forensic justification? In what respect, then, does the reality of the believer's union with Christ establish the inadmissibility of such contemporary innovations in doctrine that tarnish the testimony and challenge the witness of the church?

The chapters that follow address these questions: the relation between eternity and time in our Lord's incarnation and his discharge of his High Priestly office; the individual's saving faith and the freedom of the Christian's will to do good and live righteously before God; the possibility that the Christian may, for due cause and for a time, lose the sense of the presence of God; and the import of the believer's union with Christ. Our discussion is motivated by the virtual unanimity on these points of the three confessional documents in which the Reformation theology was given definitive expression in seventeenth-century England. They are the *Westminster Confession of Faith* (1647), the *Savoy Declaration of Faith* (1658), and the *Second London (Baptist) Confession* (1689). Those confessional statements each made declarations regarding the capacity of the human will in the state of sin, the divine decree and accomplishment of redemption, and the progress of sanctification in the Christian life.

Consider, first, the doctrine of the sinner's justification before God. That doctrine, it is by now well known, has become the center of extensive and disturbing debate within the evangelical and Reformed church. The expansive literature of the so-called New Perspective on Paul, the elabo-

---

4. Westminster Shorter Catechism, Question 34.

ration of its aims and claims, and that of the Federal Vision theology, is worthy of close inspection but cannot be discussed at length at this time.[5] The doctrine of justification, however, which has properly been referred to as "the article of faith that decides whether the church is standing or falling,"[6] lies at the center of all that has to be said regarding the revelation of the Christian faith.[7] For the question of Job of old remains imperative, "how should man be just with God?" (Job. 9:1). And the apostolic response is spread liberally in, for example, Paul's letters to the Roman and Galatian churches: "Therefore we conclude that a man is justified by faith without the deeds of the law" (Rom. 3:28), by faith alone and without contribution from individual works; and "that no man is justified by the law in the sight of God, it is evident; for, The just shall live by faith" (Gal. 3:11).

The Confessions we have cited put the question of justification in the following terms: "God did, *from all eternity*, decree to justify all the elect; and Christ did, *in the fulness of time*, die for their sins, and rise again for their justification; nevertheless they are not [personally] justified, until the Holy Spirit doth *in due time* actually apply Christ unto them."[8] In the light of that statement it will be necessary in the following chapters to examine first, the relation between eternity and time that the confessions envisage, and second, the uniqueness of the High Priestly work of Christ that provides the ground of the believer's justification.

The second of the questions we shall address, that of the nature and efficacy of saving faith and its place as the instrumental cause of salvation, will require a slightly extended comment on the respects in which the relevant doctrines have been understood in the history of the church. The doctrine of man's natural state, and the inroads to the church's theology of the philosophic assumption of the autonomy of man, particularly as

5. See Waters, *Justification and the New Perspectives* and *Federal Vision*; Venema, *Getting the Gospel Right* and *The Gospel of Free Acceptance*; Clark, ed., *Covenant, Justification, and Pastoral Ministry*; Eveson, *The Great Exchange*. A more detailed discussion of relevant doctrines will follow in chapter 7.

6. See Packer, "Introductory Essay" in James Buchanan, *Justification*, vii. The original statement is attributed to Martin Luther. John Calvin referred to the doctrine of justification as "the main hinge on which religion turns," *Institutes*, vol. 1, 726.

7. For a definitive nineteenth-century exposition that has not been improved upon see Buchanan, *Justification*.

8. Westminster Confession, XI, 4, italics added. The word "personally" in brackets is added by the Savoy Declaration and the Second London (Baptist) Confession, italics added.

that has come down through the eighteenth-century Enlightenment, will be seen to be directly relevant. It is of no little importance to observe that whereas the church's doctrine of Christology was settled at an early date, issues of anthropology did not receive a similar settlement and have been the source of diverging views in the history of doctrine.

The third of our questions, that of the Christian believer's freedom from the bondage of sin and the possibility of his obedience to the law of righteousness, is stated in similar terms in the three confessions as follows: "When God converts a sinner, and translates him into the state of grace, he freeth him from his natural bondage under sin, and by his grace alone enables him freely to will and to do that which is spiritually good; yet so as that, by reason of his remaining corruption, he doth not perfectly nor only will that which is good, *but doth also that which is evil.*"[9] At that point the paradox of the Christian life emerges. The new believer in Christ is a saint, as is repeatedly declared in the New Testament letters (Eph. 1:1; Phil. 1:1; Col. 1:2), and he is also a sinner. Our discussion will therefore bring into prominence the Christian's status and the character of his new nature and standing in Christ that it implies, and what it is that permits and occasions the "evil" as well as the "good" that the confessional statements have contemplated.

The fourth question, which addresses the possibility of the true believer's loss of the light of the countenance of God, has been raised by the confessions in the manner already stated and in the following larger context: "God doth continue to forgive the sins of those that are justified; and although *they can never fall from the state of justification,* yet they may by their sins fall under God's fatherly displeasure, and [thereby forfeit] the light of his countenance . . ."[10] Coming to prominence is a question that will be paramount in the following chapters, namely that a distinction is to be drawn between the declaration of God that those whom he gave to Christ to redeem "can never fall from the state of justification," and the reality within the Christian life and walk that the light of God's countenance may for good reason be withdrawn from them.

From the fifth of these questions it follows that if, as the Scriptures abundantly declare, the believer is joined to Christ in an indissoluble union, then nothing can be said that points to the possibility that his eter-

---

9. Westminster/Savoy/Baptist Confessions, IX, 4, italics added.

10. Ibid., XI, 5, italics added.

nal security can be in doubt or that it turns on anything other than the once-for-all imputed righteousness of Christ. We shall return to the fuller implications of that conclusion.

THE WAY AHEAD

The foregoing has established the context in which the following discussions will proceed. A number of conclusions can be stated briefly. First, the mystery of our Lord's incarnation makes it necessary to consider the respect in which, in order that the Second Person of the Godhead might take a sinless human nature into union with his divine nature, the entailment of sin that accrued from Adam's fall to all those "descending from his by ordinary generation"[11] should be broken. The cleansing work of the Holy Spirit was engaged at that point. Further, the reality of Christ's divine and human natures provides the conclusion that no communication of properties existed between them. In terms that will be explored further, there was not, at the incarnation, any commingling of the eternal and the temporal. And it follows, as a result, that there was no commingling of the eternal and the temporal at the death of Christ. It was in his human nature, that is, that he died for his people. But it will be seen also that as our Lord took a sinless human nature into union with his divine nature he did not thereby become a human person, because the human nature "was not personalized."[12] It is in that human as well as divine nature that he now discharges his heavenly High Priestly office. In the sympathy for his people that is involved in his priestly office, his human nature actively informs his understanding of his people's condition and outcomes.

Second, our examination of the nature of regenerate personhood will make it clear that "if any man be in Christ, he is a new creature; old things are passed away; . . . all things are become new" (2 Cor. 5:17). When that newness of nature is explored, with emphasis on what will be termed the integral personhood of the individual who is renewed by the grace of God, the question will be raised whether there exists within the regenerate person both an old or sinful nature and a new or godly nature. That question will be answered in the negative, and a fairly extensive but erroneous claim to the contrary in parts of the evangelical church's testimony will be examined. It will be seen that by the renewing, regenerating grace of the

11. Westminster Shorter Catechism, Question 16.
12. Berkhof, *Systematic Theology*, 322.

Holy Spirit the individual to whom that grace is sovereignly conveyed is definitively transferred from the realm of sin, condemnation, and death to that of righteousness, justification and life. God the Father, the Colossian text states, "hath delivered us from the power of darkness, and hath translated us into the kingdom of his dear Son" (Col. 1:13). That transference is a definitive transference that establishes the new-born child of God in a vital and indissoluble union with Christ.

Third, when it is seen that God can, and that as occasion warrants he does, withdraw the light of his countenance from his people, the remedies that are consistent with the believer's progress in sanctification will be recognized. But more particularly, the meaning, the significance, and the occasions of sin in the life of the believer will be observed and the respects in which the believer's sin replicates that of our first parents will be seen. For the essence of Adam's sin was that he made the false and damning assertion of autonomy against God. That assertion of autonomy had reference to the levels of being, knowledge, and behavior. And it is again the essence of the believer's sin that he falls subject to the assumption that on all such levels he can proceed independently of the God who in Christ has saved him. It is the sin of imagining that as to the possibilities of correct knowledge and right behavior the individual can establish his own criteria, or find those criteria within his social and cultural milieu. It is the imagination that one can live safely as a branch severed from the vine. It is the sin of assumed autonomy. Such a sin, subtle and perhaps for a time unrecognized, is unworthy of the Christian's high calling in Christ to whom he is joined.

It will throw light on our fuller examination of these questions to look in the following chapter at the terms and conclusions of the gospel of grace as the word of God has set it forth. The sovereignty of God in salvation, in all aspects of salvation including the sinner's justification and the saints' sanctification, will become clear. It is by the sovereign administration of God that Christ is made unto his people "wisdom, and righteousness, and sanctification, and redemption" (1 Cor. 1:30).

2

The Gospel of Grace

THE CHRISTIAN MIND, IN an age of cultural decay that edges alarmingly to a new paganism, is challenged to assert its commitment to the biblical doctrines of redemption, the state of sin that made redemption necessary, the sovereignty of God in salvation, and the demand for godliness in life. What is believing faith, what does the endowment of faith convey and demand as to belief and life, what is it in which the security of eternal destiny exists, and what is the conjunction of faith and human reason in the adjudication of claims to truth? The questions multiply. They press with new urgency in our time.

During the four hundred years of modernism in thought since the birth of rationalism in the seventeenth century, the competence of reason to articulate validity-criteria of claims to truth was more or less universally assumed. But that so-called modernism has turned into a philosophic grab-bag in which the very possibility of truth is at a discount. Anyone's truth is now as good as anyone else's truth. As to criteria of knowledge and its validity, we have arrived in contemporary culture at the point at which the only admissible absolute is the insistence that there is no admissible absolute. In that, the claim is self-defeating. But it is in that new and challenging intellectual milieu that the Christian confession is called to make its stand. What, to repeat the question, is saving faith, and how is the capacity and function of reason to be differently understood in man's regenerate as distinct from his unregenerate state? For man, created as the image of God, fallen by reason of his assertion of autonomy against God, and renewed by God's sovereign intervention, is set to work out in this life the implications of God's revivifying grace as that comes to him in salvation. He is set to pursue in the light of that his preparation for the life to come. If, as our title has asserted, "God converts a sinner," what, then, is the obligation and possibility of a righteous and God-honoring life on the part of the sinner whom grace has redeemed?

We have already referred to the Reformation theology as that received its definitive English language expression in the seventeenth century. A more conscious biblical commitment on the levels of the questions we have raised has followed from the Reformation and the subsequent expansion of its doctrinal achievements. That important movement can be seen as a significant watershed in the history, not only of the church, but of the world. It stirred Europe in the sixteenth century and had formative influence not only on evangelical theological doctrine but also on the development of culture in Western civilization. But the understanding of the Reformation is inadequate if it is not seen as primarily and essentially a theological movement. Certainly, influential forces had by that time spread from the bequest of the preceding recovery of learning that became known as the Renaissance. That latter movement, which in varied expressions spanned the thirteenth to the fifteenth centuries, projected its influence in clearly significant ways. At a minimum, important bequests came from the Renaissance rediscovery of ancient texts, its rehabilitation of the importance of the individual in the ordinary, the economic, and the cultured affairs of life, its impulse to the consolidation of a new and ascendant humanism, the invention of the printing press that accompanied and facilitated it, and its emphasis on a new openness of enquiry. But the Reformation that followed was primarily theological in its origin and its impact.

The Reformation's primary concern, and the reason why its significance and influence expanded through the centuries that followed, was with questions that impacted the ordinary affairs of the life of the ordinary man. Those questions addressed his status, his prospects in the world, and his expectation of the life to come. Two issues were paramount. First, in all of the affairs of life God, the eternal, holy, transcendent, and immanent God, was sovereign and was working out an eternal purpose for his own glory and for the good of his people, the church that he gave to his Son to redeem. That purpose, for which God created the world and for which he established his redemptive decree, was that in and by it all his Son might be eternally glorified. Jonathan Edwards was undoubtedly insightful and correct in his conclusion that the end for which God created the world was that there might be "an emanation of his own infinite fullness . . . the emanation itself was aimed at by him as a last end of the creation."[1] That objective was to be accomplished and displayed by the Son of God who came from the Father's eternal bosom to be our redeemer. On the completion of that redemptive work he would be glorified with an exaltation that gave him "a name that is above every name; that at the name of Jesus every knee should bow . . . and that every tongue should confess that Jesus Christ is Lord, to the glory of God the Father" (Phil. 2:9–11). Our Lord's high priestly prayer would be answered: "I have finished the work which thou gavest me to do. And now, O Father, glorify thou me with thine own self with the glory which I had with thee before the world was" (John 17:4–5).

The second of the Reformation issues was that a reconciliation with God was possible only because God had taken the initiative in designing and decreeing a redemption from sin. To accomplish that redemption, the Second Person of the Godhead came into the world as Jesus Christ to be the sinner's substitute in obedience to the law of God and in paying in his death the penalty for the sinner's having broken that law. That was necessary because the state in which man existed after Adam's fall was such that, though by his fall be was disabled from doing so, he remained under obligation to live in obedience to the law of life that God had set forth in his primeval covenant with our first parents. In its recognition of those facts the Reformation, in its formulation of theological doctrine, stood for the glory of God in the salvation of sinners. That is why Luther's insistence on justification by faith alone and the elaboration by numerous writers of God's predestinating covenantal designs—for example Zwingli, Bullinger, Calvin, Ursinus, Olevianus, Turretin—contributed to a consolidation of protestant doctrine that flowered in the centuries that followed. The focus of our discussion in the chapters that follow will be on those two Reformation emphases, the sovereignty and glory of God and the salvation of sinners by the redemptive grace of God.

It is true, of course, and it should be acknowledged at the outset, that the Reformation of the sixteenth century spilled its bequest of benefit to the political, economic, social, and cultural betterment of Western civilization. To understand the processes and results of that achievement is an undisputed challenge to the serious historian. But it is true, we may safely say, that at this time that civilizing benefit is wearing thin, alarmingly thin,

---

1. Edwards, *The End for which God Created the World*, in Piper, *God's Passion for His Glory*, 151.

and we now live in a climate of cultural dissolution. To the extent that is so, the more it is necessary to see that in the intellectual upheaval of the sixteenth century at the hands of the scholars of Wittenberg, Zurich, and Geneva, the sovereignty of God engineered what was primarily a theological revival and Reformation. For what the Reformation did in its theological achievement was to transmute the semi-Pelagianism of Rome back to a biblically faithful doctrine and system of belief. And to that, all other influences and benefits, along with the liberating energies they released, are due by direct or indirect causation.

It is necessary to say that the cultural decay that offends the reflective mind has not left the church unaffected. We shall return to the reasons why that is so. But there is cause to fear that we in the church have wasted our birthright in alarming degree. We say that we have been called into the fellowship of the church that Christ has redeemed, but we are hesitant to understand what his church is, and what are the terms of the covenant of grace by which it stands. We have covenanted to fulfill certain obligations that we assumed at entry to membership of the church in its visible form, but we too often regard the church as a societal entity, the voluntariness of whose membership excuses us from its more rigorous and insistent demands. We are saved as God brings us to faith individually. We are individually responsible and accountable to God our maker, judge, and redeemer. But too readily that individuality gives us cause to act individualistically within the church, to the loss of the demands of the solidarity to which we have been called and admitted.

We are too often reluctant to submit to the consistent search of the Word of God and to hear that Word preached. We too easily forget to ponder the love of the saints. We have neglected a true understanding of the grace of the sacraments. We too readily allow the importation to the church of the thought-forms and the behavior-norms of the world. We bend to the culture of the world and fail to realize that by his saving grace God has introduced us to a distinctively different culture, the culture of the church that is informed by the understanding that we live and work out our eternal destiny under the sovereign grace and will and mandates of God. We fail to think out under the guidance of God's Word what are the necessary marks of that distinctive culture. We know that the church is in the world to bear witness to the good news of the gospel of grace, but we fail to be alarmed at the fact that the world is in the church. In short, we are reluctant to be conformed to the mandates of the biblical data regarding the form, the sacraments, the discipline, and the purity of the church of God of which we are privileged to have been made a part.

THE CONSOLIDATION
OF THE REFORMATION THEOLOGY

In the seventeenth-century, an important theological literature provided the context within which the confessional declarations we have referred to were produced. Prominent in the production of that literature were such Puritan scholars as Owen, Goodwin, Gurnall, Brooks, Boston, Flavel and others too numerous to be listed at length at this point.[2] They expanded at length the doctrines of creation, fall, and redemption. The work they produced focused on the glory of God revealed in the Person of Christ and in the efficacy of Christ's atoning sacrifice. The details are rich in their clarification of biblical doctrine. It disclosed clearly that all mankind following Adam's fall stood in a condition of estrangement from God and in urgent need of reconciliation with God if the warrant of eternal perdition due to sin was to be overturned and vacated. That reconciliation was available by the grace of God set forth in Christ. Prominent in the literature of the period was John Owen's *The Death of Death in the Death of Christ*, in which he reviewed the biblical doctrines of the atonement of Christ and the extent of the benefits that accrue from it for those who were the subjects of God's decree to redeem.

If, then, salvation from sin is due to the sovereign and redeeming grace of God, the question presses as to why redemption was necessary. What was it that fractured the initial harmony between God and man and has for all time since determined the condition of sin to which redemption was addressed? The necessity of God's initiative and action in the sinner's conversion is clear on the very surface of the Scriptures, as they address both man's fallen condition and the means of rescue and relief that God has provided. The reality is that our first parent, Adam, was created in a state of holiness and righteousness from which he fell by his assumption of autonomy from God his maker. By his fall, by his capitulation to the satanic deception, and by his repudiation of his covenantal

---

2. Works by the authors referred to have been published by the Banner of Truth Trust, Edinburgh, Scotland. In the judgment of the present writer Thomas Boston's *Human Nature in its Fourfold State* is one of the most significant and useful volumes that sum up the Puritan theology which had flourished in the preceding seventeenth century.

obligations to God, he placed himself under slavery to Satan and sin. The biblical doctrines of man as created and as fallen stand prominently at the entrance to our subject.

MAN CREATED AND FALLEN

Our first parent, Adam, was created as the image of God. "Let us make man in our image, after our likeness," God had said. "So God created man in his own image . . . male and female . . . And God blessed them, and God said unto them, Be fruitful, and multiply, and replenish the earth, and subdue it; and have dominion . . . over every living thing" (Gen. 1:26–28).[3] As the image of God, Adam was created in a state of knowledge, righteousness, and holiness (Eph. 4:24; Col. 3:10). Creation, as it came from the hands of God, was covenantally structured and stood in a covenantal relation with God. As the twentieth-century theologian-apologist, Cornelius Van Til, has observed, "Scripture thinks of man as a covenant being."[4]

The primeval covenant of God with man, referred to as the covenant of creation or alternatively as the covenant of works, contained within it divine promises whose outcome turned on the condition of probation in which Adam was established. That probation was clearly articulated: "And the Lord God commanded the man, saying, Of every tree of the garden thou mayest freely eat; But of the tree of the knowledge of good and evil, thou shalt not eat of it; for in the day that thou eatest thereof thou shalt surely die" (Gen. 2:16–17). Along with the promise of death in the event of his disobedience, the covenant of works contained in its essence the promise that if Adam sustained his probation his works of obedience would be rewarded with confirmation in holy state and entrance to eternal life. The remarkable truth inherent in the covenant of works is that, as the early Reformed theologian, Herman Witsius, states it, "God has, by his promises, made himself a debtor to man. Or, to speak in a manner more becoming God, he was pleased to make his performing his promises, a debt to himself, to his goodness, justice, and veracity."[5] Similarly, Charles Hodge, the nineteenth-century Princeton theologian, observes that "Had he [Adam] retained his integrity he would have merited the promised

3. See the fuller discussion of man as the image of God in Vickers, *Christian Confession*, ch. 3.

4. Van Til, *Apologetics*, 27.

5. Witsius, *Economy of the Covenants*, vol. 1, 48.

blessing."[6] The conditional promise to Adam contemplated his confirmation in righteousness and the reward of eternal life in the event of his obedience. That conclusion, that Adam would have merited the promised reward, is confirmed by the outcome of the Second Adam's (Christ's) obedience. That Christ was rewarded on the grounds of the merit of his obedience (Rom. 5:19), his active and his passive obedience, his impeccable substitutionary life and his death, confirms the corresponding promise to Adam. For the first Adam was a type of the second.

The second Adam, Christ, the gospel of grace announces, merited by his obedience what the first Adam would have merited by *his* obedience. The second Adam, who came into the world as our substitute prophet, priest, and king, accomplished for us what, under the covenant of works, we were obligated to do but what, by reason of our participation in the effects of Adam's fall, we could not do for ourselves. Christ did what Adam did not. And in so doing he merited for us what Adam had been conditionally promised. Because of Christ's substitutionary work, God looks on us as though we ourselves had actually performed the obedience. Christ's merit is transferred to us by imputation. In that, we merit through Christ what Adam would have merited. God graciously bound himself to give us what we have merited through Christ, just as he promised to give Adam what he could have merited by his obedience.

In what we shall see as God's gracious and sovereign act of justification of the "ungodly" for whom Christ died (Rom. 5:6), he imputes to the sinner the full merit of the substitutionary life and work of Christ. In his declarative, forensic, judicial statement of justification God places "the perfect obedience and full satisfaction of Christ"[7] to the sinner's account. The remarkable result is that by reason of that imputation, the imputation of the righteousness of Christ in his active and passive obedience, God now looks on the sinner as though he himself had actually kept the law of God perfectly and as though he had actually atoned for his law-breaking.

The obedience and satisfaction of Christ is to be seen against the pristine covenant of works that involved the twofold promise of blessing and benediction in the event of Adam's obedience, and that of curse and malediction in the event of his disobedience. That, it can be seen on a more extensive examination of God's covenantal relations with man,

6. Hodge, *Systematic Theology*, vol. 2, 364.
7. Westminster Larger Catechism, Question 70.

reveals the nature of God's repeated covenants. Blessing and benediction are promised in response to obedience, and curse and malediction in response to disobedience.[8] Those promises were confirmed in various ways within the Scriptural record.

First, the promise to Adam of confirmation in righteous moral state and entrance to eternal life was confirmed by God's having given him the sacrament of the tree of life. Turretin, a Reformed theologian and successor to Calvin in the seventeenth century, observes that "It [the tree of life] was a sacrament and symbol of the immortality which would have been bestowed on Adam if he had persevered in his first state . . . As often as he tasted its fruit, he was bound to recollect that he had life not from himself, but from God."[9] Then at a later time, when God established his covenant with Abraham he instituted the sacrament of circumcision as the sign and seal of the covenant. That sacrament, it should be noted, was not intended to serve primarily as a sign of national identity. Primarily and essentially, circumcision had an intensely spiritual significance and was a sign and a seal of the covenant of grace (compare Rom. 4:11). The fact that circumcision was a blood sign portended that in the event that the individual recipient of the sign should not be faithful to the covenantal obligations that circumcision established but should in due course repudiate them, he would suffer the penalty of curse and malediction that his disobedience warranted. At the same time, the sacrament of circumcision held within it the promise of blessing in response to covenantal faithfulness.

The same duality of promises carries over to the sacrament of baptism in the current church age. The church constitutes the new form of administration of the covenant of grace. As Peter states it in his first epistle, "Ye [the church] are a chosen generation . . . a holy nation," applying the designation that God gave to his church in the earlier dispensation, "a holy nation" (1 Pet. 2:9; compare Ex. 19:6). But because we see in the Scriptures the revelation of the unity and continuity of the church from its Old Testament to its New Testament forms, we see also the manner in which the sacraments of the earlier administration are types of what are fulfilled in the antitypes of the new administration. Baptism, the antitype of the earlier sacrament of circumcision, stands in parallel with that ear-

---

8. For a discussion of the covenant of works as originally established and the treatment of it in contemporary theology, including responses to certain misplaced dissents from it, see Vickers, *Divine Redemption*, chs. 2 and 3.

9. Turretin, *Institutes*, vol. 1, 581.

lier sacrament as to its meaning and promises. It conveys the promise of blessing in response to the fulfillment of the covenantal obligations associated with it. And the water of baptism is a sign, not only of the cleansing from pollution that is of the essence of the believer's sanctification, but also of potential malediction and judgment in the event that the beneficiary of the sacrament should repudiate his or her covenantal obligations and be found to be apostate.

The outcome of Adam's probation is all too clear. But as Adam was established as the representative or the federal head of the race, all those "descending from him by ordinary generation"[10] were implicated in his action. Adam was not simply or only a private person. He was a public person, in that his posterity were represented in him. In short, the reality, the explanation of the condition of all individuals since Adam's fall, is that when Adam sinned, we all sinned. We sinned in him (Rom. 5:12). "In Adam all die" (1 Cor. 15:22). The Scriptural indictment is clear. Before the Noahic flood "God saw that the wickedness of man was great in the earth, and that every imagination of the thoughts of his heart was only evil continually" (Gen. 6:5). The same indictment was conveyed to God's people repeatedly by the prophets. "The heart is deceitful above all things, and desperately wicked; who can know it?" (Jer. 17:9). And the Psalmist again states the case: "The Lord looked down from heaven upon the children of men, to see if there were any that did understand, and seek God. They are all gone aside, they are altogether become filthy; there is none that doeth good, no not one" (Ps. 14:2–3). The apostle confirms the condemnation, "All have sinned, and come short of the glory of God" (Rom. 3:23).

The doctrinal statement is that the guilt of Adam's first sin was imputed to all those who came after him, except, that is, the Son of God who, being born of a woman, became man for our redemption. The outcome is encapsulated in the Westminster Shorter Catechism when it asks, "Did all mankind fall in Adam's first transgression?" It answers: "The covenant being made with Adam, not only for himself, but for his posterity, all mankind, descending from him by ordinary generation, sinned in him, and fell with him, in his first transgression."[11]

Here we have before us the beginning of the important biblical doctrine of imputation. "Imputation" means simply placing to one's account,

---

10. Westminster Shorter Catechism, Question 16.

11. Idem.

and a threefold imputation takes us to the heart of the gospel of grace. First, as has been seen, the guilt of Adam's sin is imputed to, or placed to the account of, us all who descended from him. Second, the guilt of those for whom Christ died is imputed to Christ who became the sin-bearer for us. And third, by way of reciprocal imputation, the forensic righteousness of Christ is placed to the account of those for whom he died. They are the ultimate beneficiaries of Christ's substitutionary fulfillment of the previously unfulfilled obligations of the covenant of works, for which they were responsible but unable to fulfill for themselves. That last remarkable imputation means that by reason of the Christian believer's union with Christ, God now looks on him as though he had actually fulfilled the requirements of the covenant that Christ fulfilled on his behalf.

We have just referred to what has been called reciprocal imputation, the imputation of the sinner's guilt to Christ and the imputation of Christ's forensic righteousness to the repentant sinner. We may note briefly the fuller implications of what is involved in the plan and activity of God in that respect. In his very helpful discussion of the doctrine of justification John Murray comments that "Justification is both a declarative and a constitutive act of God's free grace. It is *constitutive* in order that it may be truly *declarative*. God must constitute the new relationship as well as declare it to be. The constitutive act consists in the imputation to us of the obedience and righteousness of Christ."[12] When we refer to "forensic righteousness" we have in view a righteousness that satisfies the demands of law, in this case the righteous law of God. The imputation of forensic righteousness means, therefore, that the one to whom the imputation is made is reckoned by God to have satisfied, or is regarded by God as having actually himself fulfilled, the requirements of obligation to the law.

A remarkable activity of God is, as Murray has alerted us to it, engaged in the imputation we now have in view. Francis Turretin has carefully stated the underlying consideration that has determined the outcome. "Christ by his obedience," as Turretin puts it, "is rightly said 'to constitute' us 'righteous,' not by an inherent but by an imputed righteousness."[13] Turretin saw that "the judgment of God is according to truth [and] he cannot pronounce anyone just who is not really just," and it was for that reason that it was necessary that "he who is destitute of personal

12. Murray, *Redemption*, 154, italics added.
13. Turretin, *Institutes*, vol. 2, 644.

righteousness ought to have another's, by which to be justified."[14] That is why, speaking of the imputed righteousness of Christ, Turretin observes further that "the obedience of Christ rendered in our name to God the Father is so given to us by God that it is reckoned to be truly ours."[15]

What is involved in God's design in his covenant of grace is that the forensic righteousness of Christ is imputed to the sinner in order thereby to *constitute* the sinner righteous. God has thus *constituted* the sinner righteous in order to be able truthfully to *declare* him righteous. But the imputation on which our redemption turns is, as we have seen, two-sided. In a similar way, God, by imputing the guilt of our sin to Christ, thereby *constitutes* him guilty. That he does in order then to be able truthfully to *declare* him guilty. He was guilty as the sinner's substitute, thereby opening the way to eternal redemption.

But of immediate concern is the state into which we all fell as a result of Adam's sin and the repudiation of his covenantal obligations. The catechism again summarizes what is involved: "The sinfulness of that estate whereinto man fell, consists in the guilt of Adam's first sin, the want of original righteousness, and the corruption of his whole nature, which is commonly called original sin; together with all actual transgressions which proceed from it."[16] Such is the sorry state to which we were reduced. Such is the state from which we are rescued by the redemption in Christ that God has provided in his covenant of grace. We must now work out more fully what that sovereign redemption means and implies for the Christian life.

SUMMARY

We have raised two principal issues as the deposit of the Reformation theology: first, that God is sovereign in all of the affairs of life in this world; and second, that the sovereignty of God leads to the conversion of sinners in accordance with the design of the divinely established covenant of grace. That result is achieved by God's sending his Son into the world, to assume human nature into union with his divine nature, to provide in his human nature a perfect obedience to the law of God (Christ's "active obedience") on our behalf, and in his death pay the penalty for sin (his

14. Turretin, *Institutes*, vol. 2, 647.

15. Ibid., 648.

16. Westminster Shorter Catechism, Question 18.

"passive obedience"). That redemption was necessary in order to restore a reconciliation between God, whose holiness sin had outraged, and man who, by Adam's dereliction from his covenant obligations, had fallen into sin and was thereby subject to the prospect of eternal perdition.

That being done, the truth of the declaration of the apostle John rings clear. "Herein is love," John says, "not that we loved God, but that he loved us, and sent his Son to be the propitiation for our sins" (1 John 4:10). John had earlier said that "he [Christ] is the propitiation for our sins; and not for ours only, but also for the sins of the whole world" (1 John 2:2). In making those statements the apostle is not addressing the extent of the atonement or, as might be imagined, stating that the atonement was universal or indiscriminate. The apostle is there focusing his thought on the identity of the propitiator by whom the atonement was made. "Propitiation" means setting at peace. As Paul observed to the Romans, "we have peace with God through our Lord Jesus Christ" (Rom. 5:1). God is now at peace with his people. And John is saying in his epistle that wherever, anywhere in the world, a propitiation for sin is made effective, it is only by and through the work of Christ, the true and only propitiator for sin in the sight of God.

But the statement we adduced from the Westminster/Savoy/Baptist confessions of the seventeenth century is precise. It is that any individual who is saved is saved because "God converts a sinner." That is the point at which we emphasize in the chapters that follow the matchless grace of God in the salvation of sinners. There are, as the confessions state, two sides of the effect that salvation produces. On the one hand, the converting grace of God frees the sinner "from his natural bondage under sin and . . . enables him freely to will and to do that which is spiritually good." But at the same time it is acknowledged that "by reason of his remaining corruption he [the converted sinner] . . . doth also will that which is evil." That is the paradox of the Christian life. The Christian believer is a saint in that, as we have noted, he has been separated by the grace of God from the world, "delivered," as the apostle stated to the Colossian Christians, "from the power of darkness and . . . translated into the kingdom of [God's] dear Son" (Col. 1:13). A definitive transference has taken place. As John Murray has put it, the believer has been transferred from the realm of sin, condemnation, and death to the realm of righteousness, justification, and life.[17] He is now free to act in obedience to the righteous law of God. He is no longer in bondage to sin and the devil.

But the believer is also a sinner. His or her sanctification is in this life incomplete. And the fact and the meaning of sin in the life of the Christian need carefully to be understood. That is the paradox that now engages us, and in the following chapters we shall attempt to work out some of its implications as they bear on the life and walk of the Christian in the world.

17. Murray, *Romans*, vol. 1, 179.

3

Eternity, Temporality, and Redemption

THE RELATION BETWEEN GOD, eternity, and time provides a significant locus of the mystery in which Christian doctrine terminates.
The consideration of the matter and the meaning of time is preparatory to
considering the incarnation, the entrance into time, of the Second Person
of the Godhead whose coming was necessary for our redemption.

Isaac Watts, in his hymnic paraphrase of the ninetieth Psalm, saw
time "like an ever-rolling stream" that "bears all its sons away."[1] But in
his reach for the meaning of what time is and does, he may have spoken
more than he intended. For if time is, as he stated it, "ever-rolling," when
and where did time begin? When and where, if at all, will it end? Or is
time eternal? These questions have puzzled philosophers and challenged
the imaginations of essayists. Paul Helm, a contemporary philosopher
and Reformed theologian, has observed in his challenging *Eternal God:
A Study of God without Time* that "The classical Christian theologians,
Augustine of Hippo, say, or Aquinas or John Calvin, each took it for
granted that God exists as a timeless eternal being. They accepted it as an
axiom of Christian theology that God has no memory, and no conception of his own future, and that he does not change, although he eternally
wills all changes, even becoming, when incarnate in the Son, subject to
humiliation and degradation. The position at the present time among
philosophers and theologians is a very different one."[2]

We are not primarily interested at present in what Helm sees as alternative philosophic conceptions and arguments. One instance of what
is involved will suffice. "Such a view [that God is in time] is characteristic
of so-called 'Process Theology', which holds not only that God is in time

---

1. Watts, *Our God, Our Help in Ages Past*, Trinity Hymnal, 30.

2. Helm, *Eternal God*, xi.

but that it is essential to God that he changes, that his own character matures as he experiences the love, disappointment, and frustration of his creation."[3] Helm further observes: "certain biblical scholars hold that . . . While they are prepared to allow that certain expressions of Scripture are anthropomorphic—God does not have hands, or feet, or a nose, though Scripture says that he has all these—such figures of speech do not extend to divine activities. God only metaphorically has feet, but he literally remembers, or changes his mind, or grows weary."[4]

It is of immediate interest that Helm has here referred both to God as he exists outside of time, God as a "timeless eternal being," and God as he came into the world and was incarnate in the Person of his Son. In that coming into the world, Helm observes, God has made himself subject to humiliation and degradation. The significance of what is involved in those correlative conceptions exists on two levels. First, what is to be said of the coming into the world in the likeness of sinful man, yet without sin, of the eternal Son of God and thereby making himself subject to time? If, as we shall observe, time is a created entity accordant with creaturely finite existence, we need to ask whether the incarnation of the Son of God involved and carried with it, in its subjection to time, an element of finitude. Our answer will be in the affirmative. Second, what is to be understood as the relation that exists between what, in eternity *outside of time*, God purposed and projected for his creation, and the experience and awareness of that *in time* by those whom he created in his image?

In a search for the meaning of time, Bavinck referred to "intrinsic time,"[5] as distinct from "extrinsic time," or time as a mere measuring device. He goes on to say that "time—intrinsic time—is a mode of existence of all created and finite beings."[6] And Cornelius Van Til echoes Bavinck when he concludes that "Time . . . is God-created as a mode of finite ex-

---

3. Idem. See also Cornelius Van Til's comment that "The most effective means ever invented by men to date by which to make themselves believe that they are not creatures of God and are not sinners against God is the modern process philosophy and theology," in Geehan, *Jerusalem and Athens*, 394. Compare the "Open Theism" theology that claims, as does the earlier Socinianism, that God does not know, but must wait to discover, the future. See Frame, *No Other God*.

4. Helm, Ibid., xi–xii.

5. Bavinck, *Doctrine of God*, 155–56.

6. Ibid., 156.

istence."[7] Our doctrinal sensibilities, therefore, echoing the fact that God became incarnate in his Son in time, force us to consider the relationship to temporality of the eternal God. God is the "eternal, uncaused, independent, necessary" God.[8] But God has assumed to himself what is temporal, he is "in time," in the human nature he assumed into union with the divine nature in his Son. That statement, as we shall see again in what follows, in no sense diminishes the deity of the Second Person of the Godhead who became Jesus Christ for our redemption. We hold to his full autotheotic nature. We hold clearly that in his incarnation Christ did not become a human person. He was, and he continued to be, a divine Person. In him, the human nature was not personalized. There was no communication of properties between the divine and the human natures of our Lord, and Christ's deity is not made temporal by his humanity. But at issue at present is the finiteness and temporality of his human nature. That remarkable reality will be seen to have implications for the Christian's walk in this life.

The essayists have paralleled the philosophic and theological enquiry. Sir Thomas Browne, a physician and author in Norwich, England, in the seventeenth century, is justly famous for his book of reflections, *Religio Medici*, in which he wrote about the mysteries of God, nature, and man.[9] The sense of mystery carried over into Browne's lesser-known *Hydriotaphia*, in which he wrote about the seemingly more mundane discovery of antiquarian urns in Norfolk. In that he observed that "Time, which antiquates antiquities, and hath an art to make dust of all things, hath yet spared these minor monuments."[10] Time, mysterious time, Browne says, antiquates antiquities. It is, as Isaac Watts said, ever-rolling. That is the puzzle. Augustine also tried to unravel the meaning of time in the eleventh chapter of his *Confessions* on "Time and Eternity." "It is not in time that you precede times," Augustine states in his address to God. "Otherwise you would not precede all times. In the sublimity of an eternity which is always in the present, you are before all things past and transcend all things future ... 'But you are the same and your years do not fail' (Ps.101:28). Your 'years' neither go nor come.... Your 'years' are 'one day' (Ps. 89:4; 2 Pet. 3:8), and your 'day' is not any and every day but Today

7. Van Til, *Systematic Theology*, 66.

8. Howe, "The Living Temple," in *Works*, vol. 1, 27.

9. Browne, *Religio Medici*, passim.

10. Browne, *Hydriotaphia*, ch. 5, paragraph 1.

. . . Your Today is eternity. So you begat one coeternal with you, to whom you said: 'Today I have begotten you'. . . . There was therefore no time when you had not made something, because you made time itself."[11]

There, at least, we have a dictum, consistent with divine revelation, that provides a firm ground for our further enquiry. Simply, but boldly stated, God created time. But it is precisely at that point that questions arise, questions that are crucially relevant to our doctrinal enquiry. What does the rolling of time mean, we need to ask, for both our Christian doctrine and our Christian lives? The answer resides on two levels, as our observations to this point have implied. First, what are we to say, if we wish to be consistent with the Scriptural revelation, that the entry into time implies for the Person of the Son of God incarnate? And second, what is to be said about the Christian believer's position and prospects in time?

We asked at the beginning whether time could be understood to be eternal. We answered in the negative. We did that because we saw that time was God-created. It had a beginning. At the beginning end of the temporal process, at its inception, it was entirely distinct from eternity. It came into being. But what is to be said of time now that it exists as a created entity? Will time come to an end? Our answer to that question, as it impacts the meaning of Christian salvation, is that time, in the sense of Bavinck's "intrinsic time," will not come to an end. Time will unroll throughout the eternal age. The editor of John Newton's hymn spoke rightly and wisely when he said that "When we've been there ten thousand years,/ bright shining as the sun,/ we've no less days to sing God's praise/ than when we'd first begun."[12]

Two relevant comments might be inserted at this point. First, if, as has been said, time as we experience it is a mode of our finite existence, there is an accordance between time and finitude that cannot and will not be dissolved. Second, in the eternal existence in glory to which, by the grace of God, the Christian believer is destined, the believer will not transcend his finitude. His eternal life does not and cannot make him infinite. He cannot partake of his Creator's incommunicable attribute of infinity. In short, therefore, as existence in heaven will continue to be an existence in conditions of finitude, so time will continue as the mode of accommo-

11. Augustine, *Confessions*, 230.
12. Newton, *Amazing Grace*, Trinity Hymnal, 460, stanza cited credited to John P. Rees.

dation of that finitude. We do not know, of course, the form in which time in the eternal age will constitute that accommodation of finitude, in the same way as we do not know the capacities for spatial movement that we shall experience in eternity. But we know that our being and our knowing will continue to be sequential.

When we say that man will not escape his finitude, we are saying in other words that he will not escape his sequentiality. We shall not know in an instant all that is to be known. We shall learn. And sequential knowing, and indeed speaking, will necessarily involve a lapse of time. Bavinck's observation is to the point: "To eliminate time from our thinking is to eliminate our thinking and hence is impossible. . . . Existence in time is the necessary form of all that is finite and created."[13] Time and space, that is, having been created, will not be destroyed and dissolved. Eternity, then, we have cause to conclude, will contain a before and an after as to time and a near and a far as to space. Not all that is in prospect has been revealed to us. But we do know, as to time, that because our Lord himself will be the light of eternity and there will be no need of the sun (Rev. 21:23), temporal existence will then not be, as it necessarily is now, diurnal. In saying that, we are recalling Bavinck's distinction between the extrinsic and the intrinsic senses of time. The former, the extrinsic, meaning by that time as a measuring device, "will one day cease."[14] It will cease to be measured by the sun, or to be diurnal with its differences between day and night. But what we have said refers to time in its intrinsic sense. We are not saying that God in his eternal divine essence is subject to time in any sense. And we are not speaking of God the Son, *in his divine nature*, as subject to time. We are speaking only of two things: first, the temporal consciousness of man in his finitude; and second, the temporality of the *finite human nature* assumed by Christ, his human nature in its faculties of soul, its consciousness, affections, and actions. It can quite properly be said that in the eternal state we shall have put on incorruption. But it is necessary to observe that incorruptibility does not, and will not, dissolve temporality.

But that is not all that is to be said. Before we proceed, we must return to the incarnation of the Son of God. We have asked whether the submission to time by the Son of God connoted an aspect of finitude. We answer in the affirmative. That is so because when the Son of God came

13. Bavinck, *Reformed Dogmatics*, vol. 2, 428.
14. Ibid., 162.

into the world to become Jesus Christ he took to himself "a true body and a reasonable soul,"[15] and it is disclosed in the revelation that that true body and soul was created, finite, and subject to all the elements of suffering and temptation to which man is subject (Heb. 4:15–16). Remarkable as the doctrine is, our Lord now sits at the right hand of the Father in that same human nature, partaking of its finiteness and temporality. For that reason we have referred in our title to this chapter to the perspectives of eternity and temporality as relevant to the grace of redemption.

Let us take up now the questions of the reality of the human nature in time assumed by the Second Person of the Godhead, and the relation between what God has decreed outside of time and the awareness of that by the Christian believer within time.

THE CONFESSIONAL STATEMENT

"God did, *from all eternity*, decree to justify all the elect; and Christ did, *in the fulness of time*, die for their sins, and rise again for their justification; nevertheless they are not justified, until the Holy Spirit doth *in due time* actually apply Christ unto them."[16]

Here we have an introduction to the mystery of God's deliberative determination of redemption. We have said that God exists in a timeless eternity. His knowledge of himself and of reality external to his Godhead, his thoughts, deliberations, and intentions are not sequential. He knows all things in one eternal act of knowing. And yet, as the Confession has said, he decreed before the foundation of the world the justification of those he chose to redeem. That plan of redemption, we have adequate reason to conclude from the Scriptural data, proceeded from a deliberative council between the Persons of the Godhead (Acts 2:23, 4:28; Eph. 1:4, 11).[17] But if it is to be said of the eternal God that there is no succession of moments, no sequences of time, in his being or knowledge, how, then, can it be said that it was a deliberative process culminating in a divine covenant of redemption, that resulted in our rescue from sin? Berkhof has observed judiciously on the point: "The word 'counsel,' which is one of the terms by which the decree is designated, suggests careful deliberation and consultation. It may con-

---

15. Westminster Shorter Catechism, Question 22.

16. Westminster Confession, XI, 4, italics added.

17. See the fuller discussion in Vickers, *Christian Confession*, 75–76.

tain a suggestion of an intercommunication between the three persons of the Godhead."[18]

That intratrinitarian communication between the Father, the Son, and the Holy Spirit led to a distribution of redemptive offices among the three Persons, each of whom is characterized by, and is to be known as possessing, distinguishable properties. In recognizing the distinctive redemptive offices of the Persons of the Godhead we are contemplating the trinity of God in its so-called economic and not its ontological aspect. As to the essence of the Godhead, in God existing in an ontological trinity, there is no subordination of one Person to another. The full essence of God resides fully in each of the Persons. In respects that do not call for fuller review at this time, we hold to the works of the Godhead *ad intra* (the works within the Godhead before the foundation of the world), as taking up the eternal generation of the Son and the spiration or setting forth of the Holy Spirit. But we hold also to the autotheotic nature of the Son and the Holy Spirit. As to God the Son, we say that as to his nature he is autotheotic, fully God in himself, but as to his Person he is of the Father. That is to say, he was eternally begotten of the Father, with the acknowledgment of the mystery at that point that Augustine observed in his search for the meaning of time.

When we say that there was no subordination within the ontological trinity but that a subordination existed within the economic trinity in the realization of the Persons' respective redemptive offices, we can say the following without damage to that conclusion. God the Son, for example, was subordinate in the following threefold respect: first, as to mode of subsistence (his having been begotten of the Father); second, as the nineteenth-century Princeton theologian, Charles Hodge, put it, in "the voluntary subordination of the Son in his humbling himself to be found in fashion as a man, and becoming obedient unto death, and therefore subject to the limitations and infirmities of our nature"; and third, in "The economical or official subjection of the theanthropos. That is, the subordination of the incarnate Son of God, in the work of redemption and as the head of the church."[19] But the veil of mystery implicit in the works of God internal to the Godhead has not been, and in the context of our finitude cannot be, drawn aside. We can only bow in worship and praise before the mystery

---

18. Berkhof, *Systematic Theology*, 103–4.
19. Hodge, *Commentary on 1 & 2 Corinthians*, 63.

of God's being as he has revealed himself and stated his purposes in the Scriptures. But the seeming discordance between God's timelessness and his deliberative decision to redeem is alleviated by the recognition that in it we have an anthropomorphism of the highest order. Indeed, it is to be said that all of God's revelation is anthropomorphic. In his revelation God has accommodated himself to our humanity and, moreover, to our fallenness from which his redemption has rescued us.

Now the Confession states that *in due time* Christ died for the justification of his people in accordance with God's decree. "When the fulness of the time was come, God sent forth his Son, made of a woman, made under the law, to redeem them that were under the law, that we might receive the adoption of sons" (Gal. 4:4–5). Two questions arise. First, why was the incarnation of the Son of God necessary for the accomplishment of the redemptive purposes that were in view? And second, what, more precisely, was involved in the sinless entry into time of the Second Person of the Godhead?

We do not rehearse at this time all that is to be said regarding the entry of sin into the world, the dereliction of our first parents from their obligations under the covenant of creation, and the entailment of the guilt of that sin to all of Adam's posterity by ordinary generation. The detailed doctrines of the imputation of Adam's sin and the transmission of his fallen nature were referred to in the preceding chapter.[20] We look, rather, at the fact that Adam's fall involved the loss of his privilege of direct communion with God. That directness of communion had been enjoyed so long as Adam was qualified in his pristine holiness to discharge his mandated office of priesthood. He enjoyed that privilege when God, in the theophanic appearance of the Second Person of the Godhead, walked with him in the garden in the cool of the day (Gen. 3:8). But henceforth and by virtue of his fall, there could be no such direct communication. Now the intermediation of a priest was necessary. We know that following the patriarchal period of redemptive history the office of the priesthood was institutionalized in the Mosaic administration. But that institution itself, as did so much of the Mosaic system, pointed to the coming of a High Priest who would be in his Person the final efficient and effective mediator between God and man.

---

20. See the discussion in chapter 2 under the heading "Man created and fallen."

It was necessary, if a reconciliation between God and man were to be effected, and given the incapacities to which we were reduced by Adam's fall, that the mediator should be both God and man. Only in that way could the chasm between God and man be closed. A highly significant statement to that effect, that forged one of the building blocks of the more expanded Reformation theology, appeared in the *Cur Deus Homo* ("Why God Became Man") of Anselm, Archbishop of Canterbury in the eleventh and the beginning of the twelfth century.[21] It was necessary, that is, that a mediator who was both God and man should appear in time, become subject to the vicissitudes of time, yet without sin, and in his assumption of human nature be like those he came to reconcile to God (Heb. 2:9–10). But more was involved in the process and accomplishment of redemption.

Those for whom Christ gave his life of obedience and for whose salvation he died, those whom the Father had given to him for that purpose (John 17:6, 9), necessarily became his property. "Ye are not your own," the apostle stated to the Corinthians, "for ye are bought with a price" (1 Cor. 6:19–20). It is of the essence of the entire conception and process of redemption that those who are redeemed have become the property of the Redeemer. It is at that point that the necessity of the coming into the world of the Second Person of the Godhead again becomes apparent. It was not possible that a man, a natural descendent of Adam, could discharge the office of redeemer. Not only did his own sin stand in the way. Not only would he be excluded from that office by reason of the necessity that would be laid upon him to atone for his own infinitely damnable sin, thereby disqualifying him from the ability to do anything to discharge the guilt of the sin of others. But most notably, it was inconceivable that any one such man could qualify to assume the property of those who were to be redeemed. That, however, is what Christ accomplished. He purchased us from the estate of sin. We belong to him. He is our Lord Redeemer and we are his property. For that reason the incarnation of the Second Person of the Godhead was necessary.

THE VIRGIN BIRTH OF THE REDEEMER

Given the necessities we have just observed, it was necessary further that the Second Person of the Godhead should come into the world by being born of a virgin. What was impossible to human conceptions was dictated

---

21. See the discussion in Vickers, *Divine Redemption*, 17–22.

by God's eternal design. The virgin birth of our Lord had been prophesied long before (Isa. 7:14, 9:6–7). We take brief note of a number of questions that arise doctrinally at that point.

The mystery and the miracle of the incarnation press upon us. Two considerations are involved. In the first place, because it was the eternal Son of God who thus became man (though by reason that his human nature was not personalized he was not a human person[22]), and that the child that was born was necessarily sinless, it was necessary that the entailment of sin that existed as a result of Adam's fall should be broken. Our Lord was born of a woman who was, again in the necessities of the case and contrary to certain doctrinal arguments to the contrary (as in Roman Catholic theology), in possession of the same fallen and sinful nature that proceeded from Adam to all his natural posterity. The entailment of that sin and sinful nature had, we have said, to be broken. How could that be done? The first thing to be said, the first respect in which the miracle of the incarnation appears, is that the Holy Spirit's work of grace in and on the mother of our Lord accomplished a cleansing from sin. It is true, and it is necessary to hold carefully, that the Holy Spirit at the incarnation did not simply create a human fetus for implantation in the womb of the virgin. Rather, the Spirit in fact impregnated the egg of the woman for the production, the unique creation, of the fetus-child. At that point, then, and in that respect, the second aspect of the twofold miracle of the incarnation appears.

We have observed the necessity that at the incarnation the entailment of sin had to be, and was, broken. If, as has been said, that breaking of the entailment of sin was accomplished by the cleansing operation of the Holy Spirit in the virgin, it might be asked whether the same breaking of the entailment of sin could have been accomplished in any other way. If, that is to say, the entailment was broken by the Spirit's operation on and in the mother, could it not have been done alternatively in both the mother and a human father? If that had been the case a sinless child could conceivably have been produced. But to say that, we would, of course, be engaging in pointless speculation. Suffice it to say that any such conception was excluded by two considerations that have been raised in our discussion to this point. First, any such pointless speculation overlooks entirely the necessity that the redeemer of God's elect should be both God

---

22. The point is well taken by Berkhof, "the Logos assumed a human nature that was not personalized, that did not exist by itself," *Systematic Theology*, 322.

and man. Only that could close the chasm between God and man. It is not necessary to repeat the argument. And second, it should be equally apparent, again for reasons that have been stated, that no human person could assume the property of those he might have set out to redeem.

We hold, then, to the revealed doctrine and fact of the incarnation of our Lord in the womb of the Virgin Mary. The twofold mystery and miracle involved was, first, the breaking of the entailment of sin, and secondly, the Holy Spirit's impregnation of the virgin. But we stand in wonder and awe at the mystery and perfection of what God has decreed and done for our redemption. Surely, "great is the mystery of godliness" (1 Tim. 3:16). Our conclusion is that no greater mystery presses on the human consciousness than this, that the eternal Son of God should take unto himself a human nature into union with his divine nature in the manner we have inspected, and that in doing so he should have made himself, for now and for all eternity, subject in his human nature to the process of time that he himself had created. He lives now in the same human nature that he assumed at his incarnation, though that was glorified at his ascension; he will come again in that nature (Acts 1:11); and we shall see God in him in that glorified nature through all eternity. The mystery we acknowledge and for which we thank our God is that in his human nature the Second Person of the Godhead voluntarily subjected himself to temporal sequences and realizations in order to be our redeemer.

We have spoken of the assumption by the Second Person of the Godhead of a finite, temporal human nature into union with his divine nature. Van Til has rightly observed that "even in the incarnation Christ could not commingle the eternal and the temporal."[23] The two natures came into union in Christ, as it was rightly understood by the Christological settlement at the Council of Chalcedon in 451 AD, without confusion, without change, without division, and without separation. The first two stated characteristics mean that the divine and the human natures in our Lord were not in any sense intermingled; and the latter two characteristics assert the full reality of the union. It is the thrust of our present discussion to observe further that there is no commingling of the eternal and the temporal in our Lord's heavenly high priestly session. We shall return to the further significance of that fact.

23. Van Til, *Defense of the Faith*, 16–17.

It is relevant to observe also that just as there was no commingling of the eternal and the temporal at the incarnation, or no communication of properties between the divine and human natures, so there was no such commingling at the atonement that Christ offered for his people. Christ died, that is, in his human nature. And further, there is no commingling of the eternal and the temporal at the point of the sinner's regeneration, the point of transition from wrath to grace. For regeneration, as we shall observe it, is the sovereign, unsolicited act of God's grace, in which the individual person plays no part at all. God is sovereign in all parts of salvation, in justification, adoption, sanctification, and finally glorification. When that is said, it is not said or implied that the person who has been born again by the grace of God has no part to play in the progress of his or her sanctification. Indeed, we shall see that it is the Christian person's failure to pursue diligently the means of grace that accounts for the failure to realize blessings that Christ has purchased.

THE CONSCIOUSNESS OF REDEEMED STATUS

The paragraph of the Confession we have cited states that *in due time* the Holy Spirit actually applies Christ to those whom he redeemed. There is a due time for all of God's sovereign works in the accomplishment of his purposes. Redemption was accomplished when, as the Galatians text stated, the fullness of the times was come. Before us now, if we may summarize for purposes of clarity, are the two time lapses that lead to the Christian believer's awareness and realization of his or her salvation. The first has to do with the accomplishment of redemption and the second with its application.

First, God worked with sovereignly designed pace throughout human history to prepare the world for the coming of his Son. That design encompassed the separation from all of the other nations of the world of a special people in whom and among whom God established a nation-church from which Christ, the promised Messiah, would come. The law was given as a schoolmaster to prepare for Christ (Gal. 3:24), and after Christ had come, "after that faith is come," or after the full plan of redemption had been revealed in the coming of the Redeemer, there was no longer any need for a schoolmaster (Gal. 3:25). Then God's special relation with his people Israel would be at an end.[24] Then the doors of the

---

24. Compare the insightful exposition of the point in Brown, *Galatians*, 128–39.

kingdom of God were thrown wide open to all the nations, the Gentiles were brought within the direct compass of saving grace (Gal. 3:14), and all the elect seed of Abraham were in due time to be brought to salvation (Gal. 3:29). The structure of the Mosaic administration, with its law code that hedged the nation in from the contamination of godlessness that surrounded them, and the message, the rebukes, and the promises of the prophets, are well known. But in the providential government of God, when human intellectual culture had reached its zenith in Greece and the ordered government of Rome had stabilized the nations, God, in the ripeness of time that then obtained, sent his Son.

We hold, then, to God's justification of sinners in actual historic time, grounded in the actual and temporal work of his Son who came as Jesus Christ. We do not hold, that is to say, to a doctrine of eternal justification. God decreed our justification "from all eternity," as the Confession states. But God's declarative, forensic statement of justification does not occur, and the sinner's realization of it does not arise, until the justification that Christ purchased for his people is applied to them by the Holy Spirit's bringing them to faith and repentance.

It is beyond the scope of our present objective to address at length what we have just referred to as the doctrine of eternal justification. But in the light of what we are saying of the relation between eternity and temporality, a brief comment will be made. Arguments in support of the doctrine have been noted by a long line of Reformed theologians, and though some have held the doctrine in modified form it has generally been soundly controverted and has not become a part of the Reformed theological tradition. The notion of eternal justification, or the supposition that God did, in fact, declare his people justified from all eternity, fails to differentiate between the eternal decree of election on the one hand, and the effectuation in actual and created time of what that decree specified as its objectives. Some theologians spoke of an "active justification" or an *actus immanens* in God in eternity and a "passive justification" or an *actus transiens* in time and after faith.[25] The very terminology and doctrine of justification became confused in the history of debate, and as Turretin observed, "Some maintain that it is an immanent act in God which was performed from eternity; others that it is transient, terminating in us and which takes place only in time and in this life. And there are some who

25. See Berkhof, *Systematic Theology*, 518, and Bavinck, *Reformed Dogmatics*, vol. 3, 591.

hold that it is postponed to the last and decretory day, in which all must stand before the solemn and public tribunal of Christ to hear the sentence of absolution or of condemnation from his lips."[26] But Turretin comments, "The decree of justification is one thing; justification itself another. . . The will or decree to justify certain persons is indeed eternal . . . but the actual justification takes place in time."[27] Bavinck, followed by Berkhof in more modern times, notes that the doctrine of eternal justification tended toward antinomianism, and "Fear of the antinomianism . . . kept Reformed theology from shifting the doctrine of justification back to that of the decrees."[28] In modern times John Murray has referred to "eternal justification" as, quite simply, "a misuse of terms."[29]

Christ purchased for his people certain gifts, the gifts, for example, of faith and repentance, and it is the undertaken and guaranteed office of the Holy Spirit to convey those gifts to those for whom Christ died, to turn their steps to see Christ as their redeemer, to convey to them the blessings and benefits of Christ's atonement, and to conduct them to glory. That being given, we have to observe, further, a distinction that is of serious moment for the Christian believer's understanding of his or her redemptive status. That has to do with what we referred to as a second time lapse and refers to the distinction between what God has purposed for each of his elect people, on the one hand, and, on the other, their actual realization and awareness of what God has prepared for them and will in due time convey to them.

To clarify what is involved in that latter time dimension, we hold to the paradigmatic significance of what is referred to as the *ordo salutis*, or the order of application of redemption, notwithstanding some tendencies within contemporary Reformed ministries to depart from that doctrinal formation.[30] We understand that the successive elements of the application of redemption stand in a logical relation as well as, in certain of their aspects, a temporal order. But what we are concerned with at this point is the difference between the time of God's accomplishing in his Son, or his actual accomplishment in time, all that was necessarily precedent to the

---

26. Turretin, *Institutes*, vol. 2, 682–83.

27. Ibid., 683.

28. Bavinck, *Reformed Dogmatics*, vol. 3, 583 and Berkhof, op. cit., idem.

29. Murray, *Redemption*, 102.

30. See Murray, idem, for a classic statement of the *ordo salutis*.

believer's benefit, on the one hand, and the believer's experiential awareness of it. A tendency to diminish, if not reject, the traditional *ordo salutis*
theology informs, it would appear, conclusions such as that of Gaffin that
"Not justification by faith but union with the resurrected Christ by faith
. . . is the central motif of Paul's applied soteriology."[31] We in no sense
diminish the importance in doctrine or in fact of the believer's union with
Christ. But we hold, in the manner of the Confessional statement that we
have cited, to the distinctive stages, or aspects of connotation, of the actual
application of redemption and the work and ministry of the Holy Spirit
in that. As to what is to be understood, to use Gaffin's language, as "the
central motif of Paul's soteriology," we find it impossible to depart from
the traditional Reformed understanding of the priority in time of justification by grace alone through faith alone in Christ alone. We do not find
it theologically or doctrinally productive to hold with Gaffin that "Christ's
resurrection is his own justification," and to speak of "the forensic, justifying significance of the resurrection."[32] By that we mean that we cannot
follow Gaffin in his doctrinal construction that speaks of the resurrection
as "the redemption of Christ," and says that "Christ's exaltation . . . is his
justification . . . the resurrection is . . . Christ's justification or the point of
entering into a state of being justified."[33] Similarly "Christ's resurrection,"
Gaffin claims, "is his sanctification."[34] That line of doctrinal development
sees the individual believer's justification, adoption, and sanctification as
coming to effect and being what they are because at relevant levels the
believer partakes of, or shares in, the redemption, justification, adoption,
and sanctification that Christ achieved for himself and, by his doing so,
achieved for those who are joined in union to him.[35] It is in those respects

31. Gaffin, *Resurrection and Redemption*, 132. See also the same author's *"By Faith, Not By Sight,"* 43.

32. Gaffin, *"By Faith, Not by Sight,"* 84–85.

33. Gaffin, *Resurrection and Redemption*, 114, 121. Gaffin follows closely the work of Geerhardus Vos who speaks of "the justification of Christ," *The Pauline Eschatology*, 151.

34. Gaffin, *Resurrection and Redemption*, 124.

35. In that respect Gaffin argues as follows: "[W]hat characterizes the redemption of Christ holds true for the redemption of the believer. As the justification, adoption, sanctification, and glorification of the former take place by and at his resurrection, so the justification, adoption, sanctification, and glorification of the latter take place in his having been raised with Christ, that is, in his having been united with Christ as resurrected. This means, then, that despite a surface appearance to the contrary, Paul does not view the justification, adoption, sanctification, and glorification of the believer as separate,

that some Reformed theologians who are working out the implications of Gaffin's conclusions now see justification as something subtly different from the once-for-all forensic statement of God at the point of the sinner's coming in faith, repentance, and trust to Christ.[36]

We have commented on the logical relation between the elements of the *ordo salutis*. The doctrine of God's justification of the repentant sinner is to be protected for its insistence on, as has been said, the once-for-all declarative forensic statement of God. It is that statement that permits it to be said that "there is therefore now no condemnation to them which are in Christ Jesus" (Rom. 8:1). "Forensic" has to do with one's relation to the law, in this case the righteous law of God. One is just, that is, when his or her relation to the law of God is what it ought to be. By virtue of the substitutionary obedience of Christ, an obedience whose merits are imputed to, or placed to the account of, the sinner, the sinner now enjoys the blessing of the state of justification. By reason of Christ's substitution, the law has lost its condemnatory competence. But when it is thus said that the justification of the sinner has been effected, it does not mean and imply simply or only that a pardon for sin has been acquired. Justification, consequent on the sinner's repentance and faith, does, of course, imply pardon for sin. But it carries with it also and at the same time the grace of God's further forensic statement of adoption into the family of God. As the catechism puts it, "Adoption is an act of God's free grace, whereby we are received into the number, and have a right to all the privileges, of the sons of God."[37] It follows that it would be a misconstruction of biblical doctrine to drive a definitive temporal wedge between justification and adoption.

A corresponding statement is to be made regarding sanctification as an aspect of the *ordo salutis*. The Catechism we have cited speaks judiciously of justification and adoption as "acts" of God's free grace, but it speaks of sanctification as the "work" of God's free grace. Sanctification is that work of God whereby "we are renewed in the whole man after the image of God, and are enabled more and more to die unto sin, and live

---

distinct acts but as different facets or aspects of the *one act* of incorporation with the resurrected Christ." *Resurrection and Redemption*, 130–31.

36. See the further reference in chapter 7 below to Gaffin's redemptive-historical theology, his concentration on *historia salutis* rather than *ordo salutis*, and his particular construction of the doctrine of union with Christ.

37. Westminster Shorter Catechism, Question 34.

unto righteousness."[38] Justification is attributed to the sinner at a point in time. There is a sense also, of course, in which the sinner can be said to be definitively sanctified at the point of justification, meaning that by reason of his antecedent regeneration he is set apart for God in a newness of life. In that sense John Murray's distinction between "definitive sanctification" and "progressive sanctification" is doctrinally sustainable.[39] But sanctification in its progressive sense is a process of renewal whereby the individual is conformed progressively to the likeness of Christ. It is the task of the Holy Spirit to so work his ministry in the Christian life that the individual will achieve that "holiness, without which no man shall see the Lord." (Heb. 12:14).

In reference to the stages or elements of the *ordo salutis*, it is necessary to bear in mind the difference between what we might call intellectual distinctions and real distinctions. In the present instance we may draw an intellectual distinction between regeneration and justification in order to understand more fully God's gracious work in the process of redemption. But having regard only to the time involved, we must be careful not to draw a rigidly temporal distinction where none may exist. For as Buchanan has observed, "no man is justified who is not renewed, nor is any man renewed who is not also, and immediately, justified."[40] There are, that is to say, no unregenerate believers, and no regenerate unbelievers. It has been rightly said that saving faith is regeneration pushing itself to consciousness. Nevertheless, a real distinction between regeneration and justification exists. The former is concerned with the work of God's Spirit in the soul of the sinner. The latter has to do with God's declarative-forensic statement whereby the ungodly sinner is declared, on the grounds of the imputed righteousness of Christ, to be himself righteous. Justification is dependent on one's faith and repentance, which are in turn the gift of God (Eph. 2:8). That faith, which is instrumentally effective to salvation, is conveyed to the person in, and by virtue of, the Holy Spirit's act of regeneration. It is necessary to say, therefore, that regeneration is prior to justification. But that is so in a logical and not necessarily a temporal sense.

Our further concern at this stage is with the place and significance of sanctification *in its full sense* in the *ordo salutis*. Given that regenera-

---

38. Ibid., Question 35.

39. See Murray, "Definitive Sanctification" and "Progressive Sanctification" in *Collected Writings*, vol. 2, 277, 294.

40. Buchanan, *Justification*, 400.

tion involves the renewing of the faculties of the soul and the implantation within the soul of a new and holy principle of action, sanctification
begins at regeneration. But sanctification *in its progressive sense*, in the
sense in which it depends on the work of the Holy Spirit in the soul that
promotes the Christian's growth in holiness, is necessarily subsequent to
justification. We therefore dissent from those contemporary theologians
who claim that the good works of an individual, either before or after
regeneration, contribute to one's final and forensic justification.[41]

THE CHRISTIAN LIFE

What has now been said of the entrance into time of Christ as our redeemer, and of the realities of the believer's redeemed state that results,
points to the question of the accrual to the believer of the benefits that
Christ accomplished for him. A significant sense exists in which *the benefits and blessings that accrue to the Christian believer are not dependent
on his or her experiential awareness or realization of them*. Consider the
apostle's statement to the Corinthians that "Eye hath not seen, nor ear
heard, neither have entered into the heart of man, the things which God
hath prepared for them that love him" (1 Cor. 2:9). That no doubt contains
layers of meaning. Given the context in which Paul made the statement,
including the accusation that "the princes of this world" did not know
whom they were crucifying (1 Cor. 2:8), he may well be stating that the
revelation of the nature, the cause, and the meaning of the redemption
that God set forth in Christ is of an order that the natural and unenlight-
ened mind did not, and could not, know and understand. That, of course,
is an unarguable truth of God's explanation of the human condition. Paul
said as much in the verses that follow. "The natural man receiveth not the
things of the Spirit of God; for they are foolishness unto him; neither can
he know them, because they are spiritually discerned" (1 Cor. 2:14). Some
commentators have understood Paul to be pointing here to things that
will become known and realized by the Christian only in the eternal age
that is to come. Calvin, however, dissuades us from that interpretation in
his conclusion that the apostle is not referring to "that spiritual blessed-
ness which is laid up in heaven for believers." "I prefer," Calvin says, "to

41. Eveson observes: "Of course, justification takes place in the context of regeneration: justification is never divorced from regeneration, just as justification is not divorced
from sanctification. Nevertheless, as justification must not be confused with sanctification, so justification must not be confused with regeneration," *The Great Exchange*, 145.

understand him [Paul] simply as referring to those gifts of God's grace that are daily conferred upon believers."[42]

In considering, then, some aspects of the meaning and progress of the Christian life, it is necessary to recall the point at which we began. We have raised the question of what is to be said of the relationship to temporality of the eternal God. In our response we have seen that two doctrinal conclusions are to be carefully held. First, God in his glorious and infinite essence, in his triune essential being, is eternal. But in the finite human nature in his Son, he has assumed to himself what is temporal. To make that statement, we have said, in no sense diminishes the divine Personhood of Christ. To the contrary, it is to understand more soundly who the Person of our redeemer is and what he has undertaken to do, and has done and continues to do, on our behalf. In making our statement we do not say that in his divine being Christ has partaken of temporality. But our task now is to consider what significance for the life of the Christian believer emanates from the aspects of the finite and the temporal in the human nature which characterizes the Person of our Lord in his heavenly session. More expansively, we are concerned with three aspects of progress in the Christian life: first, the benefits that accrue to the Christian and which may or may not be consciously realized to higher or lesser degrees; second, the responsibilities laid upon the Christian for the assimilation of those benefits; and third, as has now been said, the significance of the temporal awareness of the Son of God in his human nature. We begin with the last mentioned point.

To consider on the broadest canvas the relation between God and the world it would be necessary to reflect at some length on God's transcendence and his immanence. By the former we mean God's ontological separateness from all of the reality external to the Godhead that he spoke into existence. By his immanence we refer to his presence by his Spirit in the world, providentially determining and governing its processes and outcomes. If an unbalanced preoccupation with God's transcendence were held, the danger would exist of falling into the theological heresy of deism. Correspondingly, an over-emphasis on God's immanence contains the danger of the philosophic error of pantheism. But God is transcendent in that he is the ultimate authority over all of the world's affairs and

42. Calvin, Commentary ad loc. cit.

eventuations; and he is immanent in that he is our ultimate environment. In him we live and move and have our being.

We take full recognition of God's presence in the world and in the lives of his people by his Spirit's ordering their days and their ways. "Without me," our Lord has said, "ye can do nothing" (John 15:5). And it remains true that "God's works of providence are, his most holy, wise, and powerful preserving and governing all his creatures, and all their actions."[43] But our immediate concern is not with the truth of those statements in and of themselves. We are interested in God's intervention and participation in the lives of Christian believers by reason of his heavenly incarnate existence in the Person of his Son. We may focus most directly on what is now relevant by referring to the heavenly High Priestly office of Christ. That involves, we may say by way of summary, two things: first, intercession; and secondly, sympathy. Our Lord is engaged in a ministry of intercession with the Father on our behalf (Heb. 7:25). The fact and the terms of that intercession are well known to the practiced Christian. It is our intercessor's attitude of sympathy that now particularly engages us.[44]

It is not only because of his divine omniscience, but because also of his perpetual existence in human nature that it is said that "we have not an high priest which cannot be touched with the feeling of our infirmities; but was in all points tempted like as we are, yet without sin" and that we may "therefore come boldly unto the throne of grace, that we may obtain mercy, and find grace to help in time of need" (Heb. 4:15–16). Our redeemer now sits on the right hand of the Father in the finite, temporal human nature, though now glorified but still not rendered infinite, that he assumed at his incarnation. In that, he observes and knows and understands our own temporality, temptations, rejoicings, and stress. God the Son, now rewarded with the glory that he had with the Father before the foundation of the world (John 17:5), observes in his divine omniscience

---

43. Westminster Shorter Catechism, Question 11.

44. Compare the insightful discussion in Murray, *Collected Writings*, vol. 1, 48–51. Murray observes: "[T]he heavenly exercise of [Christ's priestly] office is based upon the accomplishment of his earthly ministry in the days of his flesh . . . . [H]is obedience, sufferings, and temptations covered the whole course of his humiliation. And it is the experience derived from those sufferings and temptations that equips him with fellow-feeling or sympathy so that he is able to support and succour his own people in their sufferings and temptations. . . . This is but another way of recognizing the reality of our Lord's human nature in heaven, and that it is in human nature that the Son of God in heaven exercises his heavenly priesthood."

all of the unfolding days of his people. But that observation and knowledge is informed also by a sympathetic involvement with his people, a participation with them in the time through which they pass, in all the events and vicissitudes of their lives.

That is so because as our Lord observes the events of our lives he knows the very motions of soul within us by which those events and the thoughts and fears and imaginations associated with them are experienced and assimilated by us. He knows, and his knowledge impacts on his reactions and his deliverances, because he too is human. He has experienced in himself, yet without sin, the entire range of possible human experience and emotions. He knows us, not only because he made us and we came from his hands, but because he identified himself with us, totally and thoroughly, again yet without sin, when he was in this world. He knows all that can possibly occur and intervene in our daily lives. The mystery of his taking our human nature into union with his divine nature remains unfathomable. Yet we know, with an assurance and conviction from which we cannot escape, that his knowledge of us now is both divine and human. To say anything less would diminish our Lord's very Personhood. "The only Redeemer of God's elect is the Lord Jesus Christ, who, being the eternal Son of God, became man, and so was, and continueth to be, God and man, in two distinct natures, and one person, for ever."[45] We are arrested by the "for ever" in the Catechism's answer. Our Lord is able to, and he does, sympathize with us completely because he is man for ever. The widening implications need to burn their impress on our reluctant souls. We have such an High Priest, one who, in the ways we have observed all too briefly, "is not ashamed to call [us] brethren" (Heb. 2:11).

We have asked what are the blessings that God has "prepared for them that love him" (1 Cor. 2:9) but of which, by reason of our spiritual lethargy and dullness of soul, we are not necessarily fully aware. The answer, in short, is twofold. God has promised that we shall come at last to the inheritance he has prepared for us (Heb. 9:15), though the glory that awaits us is, of course, hidden from us in its full splendor and significance. It is true that the Christian is an eschatological person. He is one who thinks, that is, of the eternal destiny which, he is assured, God has prepared for those whom he has purchased in Christ. The "Golden Chain" of biblical data and promise entices his faithfulness. He knows that those

---

45. Westminster Shorter Catechism, Question 21.

whom God foreknew, who were the subjects of his predestinating decree, those he would in due time "conform to the image of his Son" because they would be "called, justified, and glorified" (Rom. 8:28–30). But perhaps the Christian soul is dulled by the subtleties of the pleasures of the world, and his alignment with the things of God is twisted by his busyness with too many distractions of this life; with things that may well be good in themselves, things indifferent perhaps, the adiaphora of life, but which crowd out by their absorbing tyranny the sense of the presence of God. Perhaps we would be better Christians if the anticipated reality of heaven more fully informed our thought.

But of immediate importance is the fact that now in the affairs of everyday God by his Spirit ministers, and waits to minister ever more fully, his graces to us. What are the blessings of which we may be too easily unaware? On the level that speaks to the essence of the meaning of the Christian walk and life, they are the blessings of knowing and communing with God. We have been reminded that Adam in his pristine holy state enjoyed that blessing in the highest degree. God walked with him in the garden in the cool of the day (Gen.3:8). And to bring the possibility down to our everyday, did not our Lord say, "I stand at the door and knock; if any man hear my voice, and open the door, I will come in to him, and will sup with him, and he with me"? (Rev. 3:20). There our Lord is appealing for the admission to our lives of his sanctifying presence and influence. But too often and too much, we don't hear him. Blessings that are ours in every sense because he purchased them for us go unrealized because we are reluctant to admit him to our lives. We have experienced surprise and wonder as we have looked back over our life-journey and seen the way in which God by his grace and providence has worked out for us more than we had, or could have, imagined. We have had cause to thank him for his bountiful blessing far above what we could have contemplated. But now at this point we are speaking of something quite beyond that.

We are speaking at present, not only or simply of knowing after the fact the blessings that God has given to us. We are speaking of knowing God in Christ himself. Did he not say that if we confess our every sin and go out to meet him, "if we walk in the light as he is light, we have fellowship with one another"? (1 John 1:7). The prospect that John articulates in his text does not refer to the possibilities of fellowship between Christian brethren, possible and highly important and more fully explained in other places as they are. The fellowship of which the apostle speaks is the fellowship between God in Christ and the true believer. That is clear on the surface of the text, in which the apostle states that "truly our fellowship is with the Father, and with his Son Jesus Christ" (1 John 1:3). Therein lies the way of blessing, the way of discovering the blessings that Christ has purchased for us and has laid up for our participation and enjoyment.

When our Lord stated in his high priestly prayer to the Father that "this is life eternal, that they might know thee the only true God, and Jesus Christ, whom thou hast sent" (John 17:3), he had in view not a mere knowledge of certain doctrinal constructions about God and the relations between God and man. The word "know" in that context carries a much more profound meaning. We who are God's people have open to us the immeasurable blessing, not only of knowing more about God than do others who are still in the darkness of sin and estrangement from him. Wonderful as that in itself is, what our Lord is concerned with in his prayer is not that we should know about God, but that we should know him. It is available to us to know him in even closer and more spiritually productive ways than we have hitherto realized.

We referred, finally, to the responsibilities that lie on the Christian believer to assimilate the blessings that God has provided and laid up for him in Christ. The Scriptural text is expansive on the meaning and possibilities of the sanctifying presence in our lives of the Spirit of Christ. The Holy Spirit whom Christ sent into the world to be our "Comforter" (John 16:7) and who, Christ said, "shall glorify me; for he shall receive of mine, and shall show it unto you" (John 16:14), waits our invitation to walk with us ever more closely. But we grieve him (Eph. 4:30) by our indolence.

We have it on the authority of God that "when he shall appear, we shall be like him" (1 John 3:2). That assurance turns on the promise that the Spirit of Christ will accomplish the task and commitment he assumed in the council of the Godhead before the foundation of the world; namely, that he would infallibly apply to those for whom Christ died all the benefits and blessings that Christ purchased for them and that he would conduct them to glory. But in the journey to that great day more fulfilling experiences of the company of Christ by his Spirit await us. We are convicted by the reflections of the disciples to whom Christ appeared on the road to Emmaus. "Did not our heart burn within us," they said, "while he talked with us by the way" (Luke 24:32). For ourselves in this seemingly ever-darkening day, what blessings we lose because we fail to cultivate his company as we walk on our way.

CONCLUSION

It is not necessary to repeat at any length the argument that has occupied us to this point. Five propositions will summarize what has been said.

First, God exists in eternal splendor and glory in the fullness of the essence of his triune Godhead.

Second, God has entered into time in the finitude and temporality of the human nature he assumed into union with the divine nature in his Son.

Third, the blessings that God has laid up for the Christian believer are not dependent on the believer's experiential awareness and consciousness of them, though it is the undertaken and guaranteed task and assignment of the Holy Spirit to communicate those blessings to those whom Christ redeemed.

Fourth, Christ, in the discharge of his heavenly High Priestly office is able to, and he does, sympathize with his people in this world and life, in a unique and remarkable sense and degree because he too is human, "both God and man . . . for ever."

Fifth, the Christian believer is assured of blessings beyond imagination if, and as, he opens himself or herself to the fellowship of Christ by his Spirit.

May we each grasp for ourselves the high blessings that have been purchased for us at no less a cost than the coming into this world of the eternal Son of God to bear our sins.

4

The Grace of Faith

WITH PRACTICED INSIGHT AND theological perception the confessions of faith to which we have referred conjoin "the grace of faith" and "the elect" who are "enabled to believe to the saving of their souls."[1] In economical language they thereby present a prolegomenon to what is at the heart of the revelation of the necessity and the *modus operandi* of salvation. For there the arch of meaning spans from the human condition in the real time in which God's creation exists to the prospect of eternity that awaits those who are the beneficiaries of God's saving favor. The Westminster Confession had already explored the doctrine of "predestination unto life" of those whom God "is pleased, in His appointed time, effectually to call by His Word and Spirit."[2] Now at the beginning of its doctrinal address to "Saving Faith" it conjoins the efficient cause of salvation as grounded in the election of God, the meritorious cause as established in the work of Christ, and the instrumental cause as operative in the sinner's faith.

But of immediate interest is the fact that the human condition is such that not only is salvation necessary, but those who are the subjects of it must be "*enabled* to believe." Why, we may ask, do we have the "enabled" in that sentence? What disability as to candidature for salvation naturally exists? And what is the nature of the address to it of God's intention as that is communicated by the Spirit of Christ? The fundamental relationship the confession here contemplates turns our attention to the manner in which its significance has been conceived in the history of

---

1. Westminster Confession, XIV, 1: "The grace of faith, whereby the elect are enabled to believe to the saving of their souls, is the work of the Spirit of Christ in their hearts . . ." Identical statements are included in the Savoy Declaration and the Second London (Baptist) Confession.

2. Ibid., X, 1.

doctrinal controversy and what it is that lies behind the construction that the Westminster Confession has offered.

What we now have before us in the confession is the twofold reality of the being and office of Christ as that is communicated by his Spirit, on the one hand, and the nature of man as he exists apart from Christ on the other. We have in acute relation, that is, the biblical doctrines (along with the realities addressed by those doctrines) of Christology and anthropology. Who is Jesus Christ in his personhood that made the communication of his grace to the sinner possible? And what, against the varying conceptions that human thought has historically conjured, is the explanation of the necessity in which the sinner stands?

SOME HISTORICAL THEOLOGICAL CONCLUSIONS

Taking those two sides of what comes prominently to view, we recall at this point the historic relation between the church's discussion of the twofold questions of Christology and biblical anthropology, of the person of Christ and the abilities of man in relation to the demands of Christ. It is clear that Satan's first attack on the new religion of Christianity was to establish doubt as to the identity and personhood of Christ. A ready reason exists why that should have been the case. For if the truth of the Person of Christ could be destroyed, then Christianity would fall to the ground. For the truth of Christianity stands on a foundation entirely different from that of every other system of thought and belief. We can have a philosophic system without the philosopher himself. We can have Cartesianism without Descartes, Marxism without Marx, or the Lockean *tabula rasa* without Locke. For the thought systems that Descartes and Marx and Locke invented depend simply on *what they said*. But the truth of Christianity, on the contrary, depends not simply or only on what Christ *said*, but on *who Christ is*. That is why Satan, if he could destroy the Person of Christ, would at a blow destroy the truth of the faith that Christ came to declare.

In the early centuries, therefore, as it came to culmination in the Council of Nicea in 325 AD, the church confronted and rejected the Arian heresy that had reduced Christ to a created entity.[3] Nicea's rejection of Arianism was forthrightly defended by the worthy Athanasius in the years that followed, and after further doctrinal debate in the

3. See Shedd, *History*, vol. 1, 307. See note 7 below.

Councils of Constantinople in 381AD and Ephesus in 431AD a definitive Christological settlement was reached in the Council of Chalcedon
in 451AD. The Chalcedonian settlement has stood ever since in orthodox
confessions, and the church has maintained that Jesus Christ was, and is,
a divine (not a human) Person. That settlement concluded, as we noted
in an earlier context, that Christ took into union with his divine nature a
human nature, without confusion, without change, without division, and
without separation. The first two stated characteristics imply that there
was no communication of properties between the divine and the human
natures, and the last two characteristics declare the reality of the union.[4]

That it was necessary that the divine Son of God should come into
the world to be our redeemer is clearly revealed in the Scriptures and has
been held as orthodoxy in the history of the church. The hymnwriter, C. F.
Alexander, has put it once and for all: "There was no other good enough
to pay the price of sin,/ he only could unlock the gate of heav'n and let us
in."[5] Anselm, who served as Archbishop of Canterbury from 1093 until his
death in 1109, spoke eloquently on the point in his *Cur Deus homo* ("Why
God became man"), when he laid down an early, important, and insightful statement of the satisfaction theory of the atonement. In doing so he
erected one of the important building blocks of what became in due course
the Reformation theology. Schaff comments that with Anselm's work "a new
chapter opens in the development of the doctrine of the atonement."[6]

But out of the early theological debates a significant question of doctrine comes to emphasis as we consider the possibility of human salvation. While the church early resolved the doctrine of the Person of Christ,
rejecting both Arian subordinationism and Sabellian modalism,[7] there

4. The issues resolved in the four early councils referred to are explored in Schaff,
History, vol. 3, 330ff.; Cunningham, *Historical Theology*, vol. 1, 267ff.; Shedd, *History*, vol.
1, 398ff.; Vickers, *Divine Redemption*, ch.1.

5. Alexander, *There is a Green Hill Far Away*, Trinity Hymnal, 256. See the discussion
in Vickers, *Divine Redemption*, 17–22.

6. Schaff, *History*, vol. 5, 600. See Vickers, *Divine Redemption*, 20–22.

7. See Shedd, *History*, vol. 1, 254, 257f., 393–94. Arius, a presbyter of Alexandria in the
early fourth century, taught that Christ was a creature of God, that he possessed divine attributes but was not fully divine, and that he was not therefore autotheotic or, that is, fully
God in himself. Arianism was condemned by the Synod of Alexandria in 321. Sabellius
was a presbyter of Ptolemais in the years 250–260. He admitted that a distinction within
the Godhead is set forth in Scripture but he denied that the distinction was a personal
one. It was modal (hence "modalism"), meaning that the Second and Third Persons of the
Godhead were only different modes of manifestation or emanations of the one God.

did not emerge a similarly agreed resolution of the doctrine of man and of the human condition. Orthodoxy since Chalcedon has been uniform in its Christology, but disturbing differences of claims and beliefs have emerged in the church's confessional anthropology. Defective anthropology tarnished the church's testimony immediately following its settlement of Christology, and the bequest of errant doctrines that challenged the church at that time has continued in many parts of evangelicalism to the present day.

An all too brief reference to what was historically involved can profitably begin with the debate between Pelagius and Augustine in the fifth century. That debate was addressed to the ability status of man as he exists after, and as a result of, Adam's fall. The Scriptural data are clear and copious and do not call for rehearsal at this time. First, the guilt of Adam's sin was imputed to all those who descended naturally from him. And second, a sinful human nature was transmitted from Adam to all those descending from him by ordinary generation. At the fall, all the faculties of the soul were affected and disabled. The mind or the intellectual faculty was darkened in that it was blinded by the devil to whom Adam had capitulated in his damning decision and assumption of autonomy (2 Cor. 4:4; 1 Cor. 2:14). The emotional faculty was depraved to the extent that man was now naturally a hater of God and fled from every thought and imagination of the being and sovereignty of God (Rom. 1:30). And the will or the volitional faculty was weakened to the extent that the natural man is now a slave of Satan and sin (John 8:44; Rom. 6:16).

The Pelagian claims saw things vastly differently. Adolf Harnack, commenting on "the principles of the Pelagian doctrine," rightly observed that "it has made its appearance in a subtle form again and again."[8] Harnack observes that the Pelagian scheme claims that "Everything that God has created is good . . . accordingly there can exist no *peccata naturalia* [sin as a matter of nature]. Only *peccata per accidens* [sin is incidental in the following sense]. . . . The most important and best endowment of [human nature] is free will."[9] "Man is able to resist every sin, therefore he must do so . . . Sin always remains an affair of the will and . . . All men stand in the condition of Adam before his fall."[10] In his larger multi-volume work on

---

8. Harnack, *Outlines of . . . History*, 368–69.

9. Ibid., 369.

10. Ibid., 370.

the *History of Dogma* Harnack refers to the Pelagian doctrine, as stated at the Synod of Carthage in the year 418, as claiming that "man can be without sin and can keep the divine commands easily if he will."[11]

Augustine argued vehemently against that Pelagian scheme. He rightly claimed that it completely misrepresented the biblical doctrine of the fall and therefore set theological anthropology on a totally wrong track. Pelagius, arguing for the freedom of the will in postlapsarian man, effectively stood for a *human monergism*, or, in other words, for a human autosoterism [man saves himself] in the matter of salvation. Augustine, to the contrary, rightly argued for a *divine monergism*.[12] It is God who saves. It is by grace alone that we are saved. Turretin, a prominent successor to Calvin in the Reformation century, treats the Pelagian controversy at length. Commenting on the state of the faculty of the will, he observes that "the question returns to this—whether unregenerate man still has such strength of free will as to be indifferent to good and evil and is able not to sin without the grace of regeneration. The adversaries affirm; we deny."[13]

Schaff acknowledges that "After Augustine's death ... the intermediate system of *Semi-Pelagianism* ... became prevalent."[14] The Roman Catholic theology, as affirmed at the Council of Trent (1545–1563), developed into a semi-Pelagianism in which a degree of freedom of the will was assumed, even if it was not explicitly asserted. In ascribing a certain freedom of the will to fallen man, the Tridentine theology said that that freedom had been weakened, but not destroyed, by the fall.[15] Trent therefore asserted that after the fall man "retained the power of doing something that was really acceptable to God, and that contributed in some way, by its goodness and excellence, to his reception of divine grace, and his ultimate salvation."[16] In that statement we have the errant Roman Catholic doctrine of congruent grace or congruent merit. Turretin refers to that as "a work morally good, done from the free will unassisted by grace (to wit, that is congruous and suitable to the divine goodness to infuse the grace of justification

11. Harnack, *History,* vol. 5, 175, quoted in Sproul, *Faith Alone,* 136.

12. See the discussion in Schaff, *History*, vol. 3, 786.

13. Turretin, *Institutes*, vol. 1, 669.

14. Schaff, *History*, vol. 3, 786.

15. See the discussion in Cunningham, *Historical Theology*, vol. 1, 576ff.

16. Ibid., 577.

into those morally disposed and doing what they can)."[17] Salvation, in those terms, becomes a matter of a synergism between the actions of man in his deserving of grace and his freedom to cooperate with grace, and the action of God in communicating a measure of grace to the sinner.

The essence of the Reformation achievement, however, is that it transmuted the semi-Pelagianism of Rome back to the rediscovery of the biblical doctrine of the sovereign, unsolicited, redemptive grace of God. But echoes of Pelagianism and forms of semi-Pelagianism soon reappeared. It came to expression in the Remonstrant (Arminian) theology in the early seventeenth century, when it was countered by the vigorous defense of the biblical faith at the Synod of Dordt in 1618–19.[18] The same defective anthropology tarnished the theology of the evangelical awakening in the eighteenth century. It marked the divergence between John Wesley and George Whitefield in England,[19] and it was exposed for its doctrinal fallacies by the prominent philosopher-theologian Jonathan Edwards in the United States.[20] A semi-Pelagian, synergistic view of man's capacity of soul and of the process of salvation is extensively held in the contemporary evangelical church.

In the light of what we have seen theological doctrine to have inherited, the reason for the "enabled" in the statement of the Westminster Confession with which we began is that the natural condition of man in sin completely disables him from knowing or coming to Christ apart from the work within him of the grace of regeneration that the Spirit of Christ effects. In short, apart from the renewing, regenerating, enabling grace of God, the individual person is "dead in trespasses and sins" (Eph. 2:1).

17. Turretin, *Institutes*, vol. 2, 711.

18. A discussion of that important episode in the history of the church is contained in Cunningham, *Historical Theology*, vol. 2, 373ff. The history of the Synod of Dordt and the contents of the Canons of Dordt may be inspected in Beeke and Ferguson, *Reformed Confessions*.

19. The Wesley-Whitefield divergence is reported in Arnold Dallimore's *George Whitefield*. See vol. 1, 307–19, 451–52.

20. Edwards' *Freedom of the Will*, which established his reputation as foremost among American philosophers, was written for the explicit purpose of contradicting the Arminian doctrine. A definitive response to the Arminian doctrine, so far as it bears on the possibility and process of salvation, is contained in the seventeenth-century work of Owen, *The Death of Death*.

THE IMPACT OF SECULAR THOUGHT
ON THEOLOGICAL DOCTRINE

It is necessary to take note at this point of a matter that frequently does not command as much attention as it should if we are to defend the faith committed to us. Let me make just a few points related to the confluence of secular and theological thought and the influence of the former on recent and contemporary theological doctrine. My doing so is motivated by the fact that not only in secular thought but also (which is critically important for our present subject) in theological doctrine we have in the post-Reformation period the consolidation of the assumption of the autonomy of man. In essence, the emergence of a heightened concentration on the individual as against institutional structures, including the church, reinforced and influenced the theological emphasis on individual competence such as we have seen semi-Pelagian Arminianism to involve.

The Reformation of the sixteenth century was the beneficiary, we have already observed, of what became known as the Renaissance, the flowering of thought and culture that preceded it between the thirteenth and the fifteenth centuries. Important bequests came from the Renaissance rediscovery of ancient texts, its rehabilitation of the importance of the individual in the ordinary, the economic, and the cultured affairs of life, its impulse to the consolidation of a new and ascendant humanism, the invention of the printing press that accompanied and facilitated it, and its emphasis on a new openness of enquiry. The new humanism turned the minds of men away from the church in a new degree, and when it spilled to the Reformation it was reflected in a new concentration on the individual's direct and personal relation to God. Leaving behind the church's insistence on the priestly function as that was explicit, for example, in auricular confession, the new theology brought to emphasis the doctrine of the universal priesthood of believers. But out of that came not only a new concentration on the sanctity of the individual, but a release of individual energies that had expansive effects in many areas, including new perspectives in art and in affairs of economics and trade.

But at the same time as the new theology took the church back to the redemptive revelation of the Scriptures, new philosophies and attempts at human explanation also emerged. In the late sixteenth and seventeenth centuries the Reformation theology came to its highest English language expression at the hands of the Puritans (Perkins, Ames, Owen, Goodwin,

Flavel, Howe, and many others, too many to mention), but at the same time there came into being the beginning of what became known as modern philosophy. Descartes, with his famous "*cogito, ergo sum,*" "I think, therefore I am," set modern thought on its decidedly anthropocentric track. Descartes might more properly have said, not "I think, therefore I am," but "I think, therefore God is."[21] The elevation of the individual person to preeminence in the explanation of reality, and the explicit formation of a new rationalism as a result, were paralleled by the consolidation in theology of a similar focus on the assumed autonomy of the individual as that had come to emphasis in the concurrent Arminian doctrines. Though the Reformation priority of the sovereignty of God and his covenant had become well consolidated in both British and continental theology (compare Witsius in the Netherlands, Turretin in Geneva, and Owen and Howe in England), by the end of the seventeenth century the influence of the Reformation had waned. It gave place, first, to the eighteenth century movement in thought referred to as Deism which effectively banished God from his world, and to the so-called Enlightenment in which the assumption of the autonomy of man was definitively established and became central to thought and explanation. It was then that assumption of human autonomy that spilled over into theology.

The Enlightenment movement stood essentially for two things. First, it elevated the assumption of the hegemony of human reason and the competence of reason to adjudicate claims to truth. It thereby consolidated an assumption that characterized what became known as "modernism" that reigned until variations of "postmodernism" invaded twentieth century thought. Second, Deism as it flourished as an element of the Enlightenment movement had banished God from his universe, meaning that he was not involved in the continuing events and affairs in the world, but it nevertheless continued to allow God's existence. But the Enlightenment in its full blush banished God from all possibility of knowledge. That was the essence of Kant's separation of the phenomenal realm in which knowledge was possible from the noumenal realm about which knowledge was not possible. The former was the realm of events and things which could be seen and touched and subjected to empirical test and therefore "known," but Kant assigned God to the noumenal

---

21. The importance of Descartes for the development of thought cannot be overstated. For introductory comments see Clark, *Thales to Dewey*, 308–24; Sproul, *Consequences of Ideas*, 79–90. Descartes' "cogito, ergo sum" appears in Part IV of the *Discourse*.

realm and therefore knowledge of God was not possible. God might or might not exist. But if he did, he could not be known.[22] It is frequently said, therefore, that Kant abolished knowledge to make room for faith. In the history of theology Kant, given his emphasis in this way on faith, has been called the philosopher of Protestantism. But such a designation does not accord with a sounder understanding of the meaning of faith as that came with and from the protestant Reformation. For Kant, his so-called faith had no basis or grounding in true knowledge, certainly not in a prior revelation of God to man. If ever there was a "leap" of faith, it occurred in Kant's formulation.

But it was not Kant's division of reality into the phenomenal and the noumenal realms, the knowable and the unknowable, that constituted his elevation of human autonomy and the hegemony of human reason. That lay, rather, in what he referred to as his Copernican revolution. By that is meant his claim that the acquisition, or more particularly the formation, of knowledge depended on the existence of certain so-called "categories" within the human mind. The mind (and for each person possibly differently) operated on the "brute" facts of reality to marshal the apprehension of them into knowable entities. The facts for Kant were therefore not so much given as created by the human mind.[23] That in itself, of course,

22. The philosophy of Immanuel Kant is discussed more fully in Vickers, *Christian Confession*, 7, 29–33, 35, 94. See also Vickers, *Fracture of Faith*, 158, 173, 178–80.

23. A Note on the Kantian scheme might be of interest and useful at this point. See the discussion in Windelband, *History*, 537ff. of Kant's *Critique of Pure Reason*. At successive steps in Kant's three-stage formation of knowledge, (1) the "Forms" of space and time inherent in the mind combine "sensations" into "perceptions"; (2) by means of the "categories" or "Forms of the synthesis of Understanding" (for example causality, unity, plurality, totality, necessity and contingency, possibility and impossibility) the perceptions are combined to make "experience"; and (3) by the use of certain "regulative principles" referred to as "Ideas" (the soul, the world, and God, which can be "thought" without becoming the object of knowledge), judgment of experience are combined into ordered and systematic knowledge of empirical phenomena. The "Idea" of God refers to the "limiting concept" of God who exists, if he exists, in Kant's "noumenal," as distinct from the "phenomenal," realm, and of whom, therefore, knowledge is impossible. In Kant's more fully developed epistemology, knowledge is possible, as he understands it, only of things within the phenomenal realm, as they are the objects of experience. The individual perceives, however, not the true essence of things, but rather an experience or phenomenon. The "forms of understanding" by which the phenomena are interpreted in effect determine nature itself. But of the "thing-in-itself," the *ding an sich*, the essence behind the phenomenon as thus interpreted, knowledge is not possible. While, for Kant, the conception of the "thing-in-itself" has no positive content, and is not an object at all, nevertheless it can be "thought." But its reality, which Kant consigned to the noumenal

stands in flat contradiction of a Reformed apologetic, which understands that there do not exist any "brute" or uninterpreted facts that form basic epistemological data. The Reformed theology and apologetic properly see all the facts of reality as God's facts, as already *pre*interpreted by God and available for man's *re*interpretation in the light of the illumination of the Spirit that God imparts.

Kant effectively established the assumption of the autonomy of man that ever since has formed a substratum for thought. It has appeared quite visibly in the doctrinal theological offsprings that matured in modern theology. But that critical assumption has assumed various existences. The preoccupation with man as the center of explanation as that was projected from Kant led to a reaction and a different form of expression and emphasis in, for example, the theology of Friedrich Schleiermacher in the early nineteenth century. For Schleiermacher, who has been called the father of modern theology, the autonomy of man was expressed in a new concentration on his feelings as well as his reason. From that point on, theology became a matter of the development of the implications of human religious consciousness, and it was followed by an influential and introspective pietism in the later nineteenth century.[24]

It is by no means part of our present intention to give a comprehensive view of the antecedents of contemporary theologies or of the manner in which the bold and determinative assumption of the autonomy of man is intrinsic to them. That assumption has continued to determine,

---

realm, can neither be affirmed nor denied. The objects of thought are the product of thought itself. That means that the objects are not "given" independently of thought, in the sense that thought about them is subject simply to the laws of Aristotelian logic, but Kant places beside the latter his so-called transcendental logic. This establishes his "transcendental idealism," ("Transcendental" refers to the conditions [such as the existence of Kant's categories within the mind that impose definition and meaning on the objects of experience] that must be fulfilled in order to make knowledge possible). But it should be noted that while Kant's theory confines the possibility of knowledge to things in the phenomenal realm and argues, therefore, that it is not possible to prove the existence of God, he also, by the same token, excludes the possibility of disproving him. In referring (as above) to God as a "limiting concept" it is meant that, according to Kant, in our claims to knowledge and our actions we proceeded "as if" God existed. The notion of God (one of Kant's "Ideas" as above) was an assumption of practical reason, not of pure reason or true knowledge.

24. See Schleiermacher, *Christian Faith* and his *On Religion*. For a review of Schleiermacher's theology and "The Theology of Feeling," along with discussions of speculative rationalism and the theological existentialism and the neo-orthodox crisis theology that followed, see Mackintosh, *Types of Modern Theology*.

in one way or another, the thought systems that followed. But we wish to emphasize the conclusion that what we have encountered to this point bears precisely and heavily on the answer to our question of why, in the words of the Westminster Confession, the sinner must be "enabled to believe" before he can, in fact, believe. That answer can now be seen to turn on two considerations.

First, it is necessary that a prior work of God by his Holy Spirit should become effective within the sinner because apart from that grace he is, by reason of the fallen state that describes him and the nature in which he exists, the slave and the dupe of the devil. We have seen that the faculties of soul of the natural man, the individual in his unregenerate state, are altogether depraved. They are not as sinful as they could possibly be and as they will be when the sinner, unless he is rescued by the grace of God, comes to full epistemological self-consciousness in the day of perdition. But the natural man is not capable of any understanding of God or any inclination to seek after and know God. Indeed, the precise contrary is true. Man by nature is a God-hater (Rom. 1:30).

Second, that deadness in the state of sin carries with it, as we have now seen, a state of mind that naturally arrogates to itself the assumption of human sovereignty. We have explored that under the heading of the assumption of human autonomy. Man, as we have seen at length in other places, is the image of God.[25] And notwithstanding his fall in Adam he remains the image of God, a rational, immortal, spiritual, moral, and speaking person. Man, as the image of God, thinks because God thinks. He speaks because God speaks. But the impact and influence of sin upon him is such that he naturally thinks and speaks what is sinful, not what is aligned with the holiness and righteousness of God. And in that state the assumption of his own autonomy is naturally ascendant in his imagination, thought, and action. That assumption of autonomy was the essential sin that in Adam's dereliction "brought death into the world and all our woe," as Milton put it.[26] It has continued its deleterious infection.

The sinner must be "enabled to believe," that is, because until the Spirit of God works a work of regeneration within him, he is not only unable to believe, but he sees no need to believe. He imagines that he can

---

25. See Vickers, *Christian Confession*, 38ff.

26. Milton, *Paradise Lost*, lines 1–3.

say with the poet, William Ernest Henley, "I am the Master of my fate . . . I am the Captain of my soul."[27]

THE INFECTION OF THEOLOGICAL APOLOGETICS

The explanation of the respects in which the assumption of human autonomy has infected theological doctrine would not be complete without a brief comment on its apologetic significance. A brief observation to that effect is the more necessary at this time because of a widespread tendency in Christian apologetics to capitulate to an incipient rationalism. The inevitable tendency to rationalism, we have seen, has been endemic since philosophy and theology both flowered at the same time in the seventeenth century. That tendency comes to expression again at the present time at the very foundation of theological apologetics. Let me summarize what is involved and provide at least a minimal indication of its relation to our present question of saving faith.

Since the time of Thomas Aquinas (1225–1274) it has been a part of fashionable thought to suggest ways in which the existence of God can be established or proved. Descartes, whom we saw was prominent at the beginning of modern philosophy and gave impetus to the anthropocentric orientation of thought, was in fact famous for his formulation of the ontological "proof" of the existence of God. That "proof" argued that it was possible to think of a being than whom no greater being existed, and that that being is God. The cosmological proof argued back to God as the first cause of all things. The moral proof argued that there is a God to adjust in another life the injustices, inequities, and immoralities of this life. And other attempts to prove the existence of God emerged.

But what is important for our present purposes is the fact God does not exist, and cannot be found to exist, at the end of a chain of autonomous logical reasoning. If, on the contrary, it should be imagined that God can be so demonstrated, as in the so-called philosophic "proofs," the god whose existence is claimed would be a god made after man's own image, a god of man's own imagination. What we are called upon by the command and revelation of God to see is that God has spoken and has said that he is. He has spoken in such clear terms that he gave his name, a uniquely covenantal name, to Moses of old (Ex. 3:14). Theological construction, then, must begin, not with an explanation of how to prove that God exists,

---

27. Henley, *Invictus*, lines 15–16.

but with, rather, the bold presupposition that God is, that he has spoken to man, and that, as we shall go on to see, he has condescended to enter into covenantal relations with man.

It will be clear that the differences of view we are now contemplating have to do with the widespread committal in evangelicalism to apologetic evidentialism. We raise that highly significant issue at this point only because such frames of thought must be seen to be offsprings of the same notions of human autonomy that we have already brought into perspective. For evidentialism sets out to argue from man to God, falsely imagining that man is capable of doing so. It fails to see that man is capable of reason and of making any statement of meaning at all only because God has first spoken to man. While it is not appropriate at this time to offer a fuller examination of the opposing claims of evidentialism and presuppositionalism, it is of some importance to take account of the following.

First, and to expand from what has just been said, the necessity of the *presupposition* that *God is* follows from a simple but inescapable underlying truth. It is only because God is, because he has spoken, and because he immanently upholds by his power all of reality external to the Godhead that he spoke into existence, that any fact, eventuation, or history is possible and explicable. All of the facts, we have said, are God's facts. There are no "brute" or uninterpreted facts. God has *pre*interpreted the facts and has endowed us with the responsibility to *re*interpret the facts under him and in the light that his Spirit conveys. It is in God that we live and move and have our being (Acts 17:28). God is our environment. It is only because God is, that human thought is possible.

Second, when we look now at the question of saving faith we are required to see that the faith of which we shall speak more fully is again not something that can be voluntarily excogitated from within man himself or, that is, a deposit of his own meditation or imagination. Because God is the origin and the explanation of all things, he is the origin and explanation of what saving faith is and does. Not only is the existence and being of God our fundamental apologetic and doctrinal presupposition, not only has he spoken to us and made us aware of all the criteria of truth and understanding and explanation as they exist in the revelation of his Son, not only is our own total being and life-journey dependent on him and his overruling ordination, but within that explanatory nexus there is no understanding of the need for, and the terms of, saving faith apart from what he has declared.

The presupposition of God and the veracity of what he has said lie therefore at the very foundation of all that is to be said of saving faith. That is because there is no source of explanation of any event or possibility apart from what God has said clearly in the revelation he has made and in his disclosure of himself and his purposes with relation to us.

But there is a final trap or subtlety to be recognized in the matter of our apologetico-doctrinal presuppositions. It is that we are not free to form or hold as the presuppositions from which we reason what we might take from a prior formulation of our own minds, or what we might adduce from the intellectual and cultural milieu in which we live. Our presuppositions are themselves provided to us by the inscripturated word of God. We are not free to manufacture our own presuppositions. To attempt to do so would cater directly to the same erroneous assumptions of human autonomy and hegemony as we have already inspected. As to saving faith, we are saved, if we are saved, only by God's endowment of faith in the Savior whom he has set forth for sinners, and whose perfect substitutionary life and work he thereby credits to our account.

THE ELECT

The Westminster Confession has stated, we saw at the beginning, that it is "the elect" who are "enabled to believe." Two possibilities are open to us for investigation at this point. God, it is known from the word he has spoken, has entered into a redemptive covenant with his people. We can look, therefore, at the terms of the covenant he has made, the intratrinitarian deliberation and communication from which the covenant resulted, and the distribution of redemptive offices among the Persons of the Godhead that was integral to it. Or, secondly, we can look more directly at the subjects of the covenant, the identity and the individualities of "the elect" whom God chose to redeem. As our immediate interest is the "saving faith" by which those who believe are brought to Christ, we need to reflect firstly on what, in fact, God has decreed and provided for in the matter of the faith that he makes effective to salvation.

We may bring these questions together by asking who were, and are, the subjects of God's decree to redeem. It is true, however, that that decree itself has been subject to varying interpretations in the history of doctrine. Differences of view have arisen as to whether God's purpose of salvation came to effect in one single covenant of grace or whether, as the

Westminster Catechism says, we should speak of the "decrees" (plural) of God.[28] It is necessary to speak first of the intratrinitarian council and agreement that resulted in a covenant of redemption between the Persons of the Godhead. In that covenantal agreement, redemptive offices were distributed to the Father, the Son, and the Holy Spirit. Those whom the Father elected to salvation he gave to the Son to redeem (John 17:6, 9). On the grounds of the Son's having satisfactorily discharged his substitutionary redemptive office and commitment, the Holy Spirit undertook to apply to the people he thereby redeemed all of the benefits of his atonement and to conduct them to glory (John 1:33, 16:13–14). The Holy Spirit conveys to the redeemed elect, as is clearly stated in the first sentence of chapter XIV of the confession that we are considering, the gifts that Christ purchased for them. The benefits thus conveyed include the gifts of repentance and saving faith. That conveyance of benefit "is the work of the Spirit of Christ . . . and is ordinarily wrought by the ministry of the Word."[29]

Second, we speak also of a covenant of grace made between God and the elect he has chosen to salvation, or more properly between God and the elect as represented by Christ. In that covenantal statement, as it came to historical expression in the covenant God swore to Abraham, God has guaranteed that a numberless host of individuals will be his people and he will be their God (Gen. 17:7). By reason of the Holy Spirit's application to them of the benefits of Christ's redemption they are called the children of Abraham, "Abraham's seed and heirs according to the promise" (Gal. 3:29). Again the Scriptural data are clear and the terms of God's covenants lie on the surface of the text.

As we contemplate the identity of those whom God has thus elected to salvation two questions arise. First, what, more precisely, is to be seen as the relation between that election and the question we have already addressed regarding the state of man in sin? Or what is it, in other words, that provides the unity to the statement of the Westminster Confession at this point? And second, what implications does that have for the objective status of God's elect as they were contemplated by God as the subjects of his elective decree? The first question strikes to the heart of the biblical explanation of the process of salvation.

28. Westminster Shorter Catechism, Question 7.
29. Westminster Confession, XIV, 1.

We make that statement because our preceding analysis of man's fallen state and the subjection to Satan and sin in which he naturally exists makes it clear that if God did not sovereignly elect some to salvation no one would be, or could be, saved. We shall see that it is for that very reason that the confession commenced its statement that we now have in view with the words, "The grace of faith." It should be clear that there was no necessity on God to redeem. Redemption and the complex of divine covenants are traceable only to, and they find their ultimate explanation in, the sovereign will of God. It is the will of God, as that was informed by his love for his rational creatures who had sinned against him, that stands at the fountainhead of all of his dealings with his people. "Herein is love," the apostle John explained, "not that we loved God, but that he loved us, and sent his Son to be the propitiation for, our sins" (1 John 4:10). God does not love us because his Son died for us. The opposite is true. God sent his Son to die for us because he loved us. Given, as we have explored it, man's inability-status in sin, his bondage to sin and his hatred of God, the possibility of his rescue and his recovery to the knowledge of God and reconciliation with him had inevitably to turn on the grace of God manifested toward him. That is why it is imperative to speak of "the grace of faith." Only if salvation were entirely by grace could there be any salvation.

A second question need not detain us at length, but is to be seen as referring again to what has already been said regarding the status of the individual person in his state of sin. The matter at hand turns on a question that historical theology has asked. In technical terms, are we to take a supralapsarian (before the fall) or an infralapsarian (after the fall) view of the subjects of God's decree to redeem? The question is not totally otiose, and we shall see its relation to the questions of assumed human autonomy and sovereignty that we have already encountered. The respective understandings at that point have been well explored in the history of doctrinal controversy and will be familiar. In brief, supralapsarianism sees the subjects of the covenantal decree as creatable persons, in that God's decree to elect is seen as prior to his decree to create. The alternative view, infralapsarianism, sees those subjects as fallen persons, as they existed in fallen state following Adam's dereliction from his covenantal obligations. We do not need to reopen all of the details. But some comments may be made as bearing on the questions we have addressed to this point.

Discussion of this particular controversy has faded from the theological literature in recent times, except, perhaps, for the attempt of Robert Reymond to revive it in his recent *A New Systematic Theology of the Christian Faith*. In that work he takes what he sees as a newly-formulated position of supralapsarianism.[30] We make only two comments. First, the very state of finitude in which we stand and contemplate God's decrees makes it necessary to acknowledge at the outset that God's knowledge of his own purposes, decrees, and objectives with relation to us is incomprehensible to us. When we say, then, that the ultimate locus of explanation of God's decrees is lost to us in the unfathomable realities of God's own will, we are acknowledging that there is, in fact, a supralapsarian element in what is to be conjured in human language as God's decrees. For nothing is traceable for us beyond the recognition of God's free and sovereign will.

When we say that, we recall our previous discussion of the status of the human knowledge capacity, as that is connoted by what we have seen as the tendency in both secular and theological thought to give obeisance to the hegemony and assumed explanatory competence of reason. It is necessary to guard against the notion that reason, even within the soulish capacities of the regenerate person, is capable of investigation into the mysteries of the Godhead beyond what God has been pleased to reveal to us. We are content to conclude that the resolution of the identity and status of those whom God has included as the subjects of his decree to redeem, or the thought of God as he formed his covenantal designs with relation to them, are finally inaccessible to us.

But while we leave the present question as unresolvable in the being and will of God, it is possible, and even necessary, to see also an infralapsarian element in the covenant of grace in terms of which we are saved. For the reality is that it is from the fallen sons of Adam that God chose to bring some to salvation. The people whom Christ redeemed by his sinless substitutionary life and work and death were fallen individuals who otherwise merited the prospect of eternal perdition for their sin.[31] It may

---

30. Reymond, *New Systematic Theology*, 488–502.

31. It is of interest that the Westminster Confession, at III, 7, draws careful distinctions between God's decree of predestination to life, his passing over certain individuals, or his act of preterition, and the decree of reprobation. The decree of preterition, or the eternal action of God whereby he "withholds his mercy" from some, is "according to the unsearchable counsel of his own will." But the fact that they are "ordain[ed] . . . to dishonor and wrath," in the decree of reprobation, is "for their sin." In short, preterition is referable to God's will. Reprobation is referable to the sinner's sin.

not be wide of the mark to say that God's decrees to elect and save are su-pralapsarian in the divine thought and contemplation, but infralapsarian in their execution and their implementation in actual historic time.

If, then, we are supralapsarian and infralapsarian in different degrees and different respects, our intention is only to recognize the mystery of God's purposes and redemptive intentions, at the same time as we recognize two things that have been explicit in what we have said. First, it is for fallen and lost sinners that Christ died, those who, as the confession has stated it, are "enabled to believe to the saving of their souls." Second, we recognize, and we are content to praise God for, "the mystery of godliness" (1 Tim. 3:16), and we avoid the fallacy of arrogating to human capacity what is clearly beyond its prerogative. We avoid on this, as on all levels of thought, the falsehood of human autonomy.

WHAT IS SAVING FAITH?

From the nexus of doctrines regarding the divine intentions and the actual accomplishment of redemption, the question we asked in an earlier chapter returns: What is saving faith? The Westminster Confession had earlier spoken at length of justification by faith, and at this time of day it is well known that the Reformed church has been troubled in recent time by certain new theologies that have attacked the truth of justification by faith alone. It is not necessary at present to enter on that important area. We shall return to related questions in a later chapter and will see again that false conceptions of human autonomy in thought have troubled the church. The confession is concerned rather to ask what is the meaning of saving faith itself, as an activity of the soul. Without addressing all that the confession says on the point, it is necessary to draw attention to a number of questions that establish the perspective from which further discussion might proceed.

First, the confessional statement we have before us is that certain people are enabled to believe "to the saving of their souls." That formulation is sustained by the Scriptural statement in Hebrews 10:39 that "we are . . . of them that believe *to the saving of the soul.*" The "soul" in that statement is synecdochical. We have there a synecdoche, a figure of speech in which a part is taken to refer to the whole. The reference to the "soul" is to be understood as having in view the whole person. If the soul is thought to be a part of the man, then the part is here taken to refer to the whole. It is to be seen and is to be held firmly in view that the exercise of saving faith as that is addressed to the Person of Christ results in the salvation of the whole person. But the related observation can be made that in order to understand the nature of human personhood it has to be said not that man *has* a body and a soul, but that he *is* body and soul. We speak more properly, then, of man in his total personhood in his bodily aspect and in his soulish aspect. The statement of the Westminster Confession at this point, then, is that the result of saving faith is the salvation of the individual in his or her total personhood, or what we may refer to as his or her integral personhood.

That more careful cognition of the effects of saving faith is confirmed by two further considerations. First, we reflect on the fact that according to the apostle's exposition in Romans 6 the old man was crucified with Christ. The objective in that crucifixion, it is said, was that "the body of sin might be destroyed" (Rom. 6:6). The reference there to the "body of sin" has been variously understood in the history of commentary, and no less an exegete than Calvin has understood the reference to be to "the corrupted mass . . . of sin" within the person.[32] But we are persuaded that the reference is not to a "mass of sin" but to the physical body. John Murray has concluded to that effect in his extensive examination of the question,[33] and Lloyd-Jones has concluded likewise.[34] The principal conclusion we reach is that by virtue of the salvation wrought by Christ and appropriated by saving faith, the remarkable result is that man in his bodily aspect as well as in his soulish aspect is no longer conditioned and controlled by sin. We may let John Murray make the point: "The body is an integral part of personality and . . . the body of the believer is no longer conditioned and controlled by sin. The body that is his now is one conditioned and controlled by what has come to be the ruling principle of the believer in his totality, namely, 'obedience unto righteousness' (Rom. 6:16)."

Saving faith, then, as the confession has brought it before us, means and implies the salvation of the whole person, body and soul. But a second point is to be made. While the redeemed believer has in this life the "earnest," the down payment, of his eternal inheritance (Eph. 1:14), he looks to the time when the redemption of the body and soul will be fully realized

32. Calvin, Commentary ad loc. cit.

33. See Murray, *Romans*, 220–21.

34. Lloyd-Jones, *Romans . . . Chapter 6*, 72: "What then does the term 'the body of sin' mean? It means the body, our physical body, of which sin has taken possession."

in the great resurrection day. The body, that is, has been redeemed, and we can say with Job of old that "in my flesh I shall see God" (Job. 19:26). But we should understand that we are speaking in that of the *resurrection* of the body. We do well to grasp the meaning of the resurrection. The body we shall have in that last great day will not be a new creation. It will be the old body resurrected and glorified after the image of our Lord's glorified human body. It is that remarkable prospect of the resurrection of the body, then, that forces the realization that "saving of the soul" in the context we are now confronting requires us to see that the result of saving faith is the salvation of the whole person in both his bodily and his soulish aspects.

What, then, is saving faith? The Westminster Confession had anticipated the question in its earlier discussion "Of Justification." Saving faith, it had said, is a "receiving and resting on Christ and his righteousness."[35] We do not need to improve on the old formulation that saving faith includes on the part of the believer knowledge, assent, and trust. We put the definition in that form for the following reasons.

First, the expression of faith in Christ that is effective to salvation, or saving faith, is necessarily based on the possession of a certain body of knowledge and it involves action based on that knowledge. That includes the knowledge of sin and repentance from it, the knowledge that God has set forth a substitute for sinners and that by faith and commitment to him sins are forgiven and the righteousness of that Substitute is placed to the sinner's account. The knowledge involved, in short, is all that is included in the fact that "God, who commanded the light to shine out of darkness [at the original creation], hath shined in our hearts, to give the light of the knowledge of glory of God in the face of Jesus Christ" (2 Cor. 4:6). That means that the object of saving faith is Christ in his Person and in the substitutionary sacrifice for sinners that he made. We are not saved by what we know about Christ. We are not saved by any particular doctrinal construction about God or Christ. We are not saved by any measure of faith in our faith. We are saved by Christ. We are saved by Christ in his Person and what he has accomplished for us as our Substitute.

Second, as has been said, saving faith involves deliberate action based on the knowledge that is now possessed. It involves assent to the truth of what God has spoken as inherent in that knowledge. That is to say, the

---

35. Westminster Confession, XI, 2.

expression of saving faith takes up the exercise of all of the faculties of the soul, or in language we have already used, it takes up the total person in his or her integral personhood. It is, again, the total person who is saved as a result. The apostle to the Gentiles was eloquent on the point in his letter to the Romans. "God be thanked," he says, "ye were the servants [slaves] of sin, but ye have obeyed [the volitional faculty of the soul in believing action] from the heart [with the consent and approval of the emotional faculty] that form of doctrine [the intellectual faculty active] which was delivered you" (Rom. 6:17).

Third, saving faith involves trust and a whole-souled commitment to Christ. The necessity of the vital element of trust has been recognized by a long line of Reformed theologians. That total commitment to Christ results in what the apostle confessed to in his personal summary, "I live; yet not I, but Christ liveth in me; and the life which I now live in the flesh I live by the faith of the Son of God, who loved me, and gave himself for me" (Gal. 2:20). The important element of trust is clearly evident in the statement of the Westminster Shorter Catechism that "Faith in Jesus Christ is a saving grace, whereby we receive and rest upon him alone for salvation, as he is offered to us in the gospel."[36] It might be remarked that the high conception of saving faith as the Westminster Confession and Reformed theology has seen it has been lowered somewhat in recent times by the work of Gordon Clark and some who are following in the theological tradition he established. For Clark, saving faith involves simply assent to the propositions regarding the means of entry to salvation that he understands God to have set forth in his word.[37] Clark has influenced certain contemporary Reformed theologians who define faith as "mere belief." Paul Elliott, for example, refers inadequately to "the Gospel doctrine of justification by faith (*mere belief*) in Christ alone."[38] But mere logical assent to propositional statements is tinged with a rationalism from which we have already dissented.

But it would be a seriously defective theology that confined the meaning and implications of saving faith to what was effective at the point of entry to salvation. Certainly, that is the emphasis that is under consideration at the point of the Westminster Confession that we are

36. Westminster Shorter Catechism, Question 86.
37. See Clark, *What is Saving Faith?*
38. Elliott, *Christianity and Neo-Liberalism*, 12, parenthesis in original, italics added.

now discussing. But faith that is genuine as to salvation is to be seen as projecting implications for the on-going Christian life. The statement that we have seen Paul make to the Galatian church speaks eloquently to the point, "Christ liveth in me." It would take our present discussion too far afield to adduce at length the significance of faith for the progress of the believer's sanctification. But we do well to recognize that the faith in Christ which, as the confession here states it, is "the work of the Spirit of Christ in their hearts," is not only effective to the definitive realization of salvation at the beginning of the Christian life, but is effective also in the sanctifying progress in holiness and righteousness to which the Christian is called in Christ.

THE GRACE OF FAITH

What, we are therefore required to ask, are the implications of saving faith that spill over to the on-going Christian life? The short answer may be that the Christian "lives by faith." The attachment to Christ, indeed the existential union with him in which the believer is established at the point of regeneration, the consciousness of that union of which the believer is aware at the point of his justification, mean and imply that henceforth his life is what it is because the Spirit of Christ lives within him. Faith in Christ, that comes to expression in the commitment that first saw him as the Savior from the load and guilt of sin, continues to inform and determine the very shape and progress of the Christian's life. Faith in Christ comes to expression, first at the point of justification, and secondly in the believer's on-going sanctification. But in the context of the confession's statements on these matters it is necessary to look a little more deeply at the existential relations that are involved.

We observe again that the Westminster Confession at this stage begins its statement with the remarkably insightful words and concept, "The grace of faith." That is precisely what is at issue. Faith is a grace. When Paul said to the Ephesians that "by grace are ye saved through faith" (Eph. 2:8), he was saying that our salvation is due entirely, in all of its parts and aspects, to the grace of God. When he goes on to say, "and that not of yourselves; it is the gift of God," he might not have been referring precisely to faith, but to grace and the entire process of salvation as the gift of God. Commentary has been historically divided on the point. Lloyd-Jones addresses the question judiciously in his sermonic commentary on the text.

"The great question is, what does the 'that' refer to? And there are two schools of opinion." One says the antecedent of the 'that' is faith and the other says it is grace.[39] In the outcome, such a difference of view is not important. Both points of view come to much the same thing in the end. We can say, however, that the position taken on the question should not be determined as a matter of grammar or language. What is relevant, rather, is the doctrine that salvation in its entirety is due to, and depends completely on, the grace of God freely communicated to the sinner. Salvation, because it depends on and results from the grace of God, cannot in any sense be taken to depend on the merit or works of the sinner. The apostle therefore adds in the Ephesian context, "Not of works, lest any man should boast" (Eph. 2:9).

We have made the point because it can be seen to throw its light on what we are now adducing as the significance of the grace of faith for the on-going Christian life. We have said that the Christian lives by faith. That is frequently adduced from the textual statement that "The just shall live by faith" (Hab. 2:4; Rom. 1:17; Gal. 3:11; Heb. 10:38). But in order to see the relation between that statement on the one hand and our present investigation of saving faith on the other, it is necessary to look a little more deeply into the text.

Habakkuk had stood on his watchtower to see what God would say to him. God spoke to him of a "vision" that "at an appointed time . . . will surely come" (Hab. 2:4). Careful reflection on the context shows that the reference is to the fact that in due time Christ would come as the promised Savior of his people. But not every individual would be expectantly ready for his coming. There would be those whose "soul is lifted up [and] is not upright in him," and for them the promised life in Christ would not be realized. On the other hand, there are the "just," and such individuals, the text says, "shall live by his faith." It is being said that there are two classes of people. But there is only one class, made up of those who have been accounted "just" because of their faith, who will realize the blessing or who will "live."

Consider the context of the text in the Galatian letter. Paul had spoken strenuously there of the fact that no man can be justified by the works of the law. Justification is by faith. The meaning of that conclusion, which is spread liberally throughout the Pauline literature, will be clear to the

---

39. See Lloyd-Jones, *God's Way of Reconciliation*, 135.

practiced reader. In its Galatian context it is saying that it is not the one who imagines he can be justified by the works of the law who will live. It is the one who has been justified by faith. In each of the New Testament citations of the text the word order in the Greek places the "by faith" before "shall live." Of course we need to be careful about making too much of word order in the Greek. But in the present case there is no final reason why we should not allow the word order to cast its light on the exegesis of the text, and there is good reason why we should.

We have addressed at some length the statement of the Westminster Confession on saving faith. We see now that it is those, and only those, who have received the gift of God's grace of faith who can, and will, realize the blessings of life in Christ. It is of interest that the recent English Standard Version of the New Testament contains a marginal note at Galatians 3:11 that gives as a translation of the text, "The one who by faith is righteous will live." But a particularly insightful and extensive exegesis in the direction we are now suggesting is contained in the commentary by John Brown. Brown comments that the text as it stands may be taken to "convey an important truth—that it is by the continued belief of the truth that the new life of the Christian is sustained; or, in other words, that he continues good and happy, and grows better and happier. . . . But we must also state that the words admit of another rendering, and that the object of the prophet [Habakkuk] in primarily using them, and of the apostle in quoting them, both here and elsewhere, requires that other rendering . . . 'The man who is the object of God's favourable regard in consequence of his faith, that man shall live, or be happy.'"[40]

We thus have a direct linkage between the statement of the Westminster Confession regarding the meaning of saving faith and the resulting effects and implications of that for the Christian life. It is saving faith that introduces us to the possibility, and indeed to the certain fact, of fullness of life in Christ. That is why the apostle could say, "I live . . . but Christ liveth in me" (Gal. 2:20). Saving faith introduced him to life in Christ.

But there is a final point that deserves a briefer comment in the context that the Westminster Confession here presents.

---

40. Brown, *Galatians*, 126.

THE MYSTERY OF THE GRACE OF FAITH

We saw at the beginning of our discussion that both secular and theological thought have frequently been misdirected by the assumption of the autonomy of man and by the correlative assumption of the competence of human reason to discover and adjudicate claims to truth. That proposition returns at this final stage. For when our Lord explained to Nicodemus that "ye must be born again," he also hastened to say that "The wind bloweth where it listeth, and thou hearest the sound thereof, but canst not tell whence it cometh, and whither it goeth; so is every one that is born of the Spirit" (John 3:7–8). There is a mystery in the divine work of regeneration that human cognition cannot corral and understand. The Westminster Confession has said as much in the context we have examined, in the words: "The grace of faith . . . is the work of the Spirit of Christ."

Similarly, it now has to be said, a mystery of divine intention and grace informs the work of the Spirit of God throughout all of the development of the Christian life until the day of glory dawns. Who can understand the moving of the Spirit? We experience, we know, the remarkable effects of his ministry to us. But who can know the timing and the purpose of his coming in all of the fullness of the divine intention? Have we never been surprised by his movement in our lives? Have we never had reason to thank him and praise him for his surprising succor and comfort in distress, his providential orderings, and his coming to us with heart-warming solace in our extremities?

A mystery informs the Christian life, at its beginning, throughout its course, and until its end. Is it not true that "great is the mystery of godliness," or the mystery of what God has done and is doing? Is it not true, as Paul adduced Isaiah's statement (Is. 64:4) in his letter to the Corinthians, "Eye hath not seen, nor ear heard, neither have entered into the heart of man, the things which God hath prepared for them that love him"? (1 Cor. 2:9). Do we not now see "through a glass darkly"? (1 Cor. 13:12). Do we not "walk by faith, not by sight"? (2 Cor. 5:7).

Away, then, with every imagination that we ourselves can plumb the depth of the knowledge or the love of God. Away with the notion that with puny minds we can "contend [argue] with him" (Job 9:3). "Where wast thou," God says, "when I laid the foundation of the earth? declare, if thou hast understanding. . . . Or who laid the corner stone thereof; when the morning stars sang together, and all the sons of God shouted for joy?"

(Job 38:4–7). God's ways are past finding out. His thoughts are higher than our thoughts (Is. 55:8–9). Away with any suggestion that our weak and finite and faltering thought can understand what God is doing with and for us. We bow before him and praise him for the fact that by his Holy Spirit he has conveyed to us, not a comprehensive understanding of his being and will and purpose, but a realization from which we cannot escape, namely that he has assumed us to himself in an indissoluble union in Christ his Son.

That is why the Westminster Confession has said that there is a "grace of faith," and that those who, by the unfathomable will of God, are numbered among his "elect," have been graciously made the beneficiaries of "the work of the Spirit of Christ in their hearts." May we in response give to him the totalitarian allegiance that he desires and demands.

5

When God Converts a Sinner

THE CONFESSIONS THAT HAVE motivated our present studies have spoken eloquently of the status of the human will, its possession of "natural liberty," its competence in man's "state of innocency," its bondage as a result of Adam's fall, and its function in the regenerate Christian life. While it is acknowledged that our first parents as they came from the hands of their Creator "had freedom and power to will and to do that which is good and well pleasing to God,"[1] in their created finitude they were nevertheless mutable, defectible, and, as was in due course registered in fact, they "fell from the estate wherein they were created."[2] The Confessional explanation of the result is that "Man, by his fall into a state of sin, hath wholly lost all ability of will to any spiritual good accompanying salvation."[3]

The Confession is saying that at the fall, as to its theological import, man lost his free will. It is not necessary for our present purposes to rehearse the long history of philosophic discussions of the freedom or otherwise of the will.[4] We may note at a minimum that a problematic central to such discussions has been the apparent conflict between human freedom and divine predestination, or that between divine sovereignty and human responsibility. The distinguished scientist, Albert Einstein, confronted that question and his conclusion provides a backdrop to widespread opinion. "Nobody, certainly, will deny that the idea of the existence of an omnipotent, just, and omnibeneficent personal God is able to accord man solace, help and guidance; also by virtue of its simplic-

1. Westminster Confession, IX, 2.
2. Westminster Shorter Catechism, Question 13.
3. Westminster Confession, IX, 3.
4. See Vickers, *Divine Redemption*, ch. 4.

ity it is accessible to the most undeveloped mind. But . . . if this being is omnipotent then every occurrence, including every human action, every human thought, and every human feeling and aspiration is also his work. How is it possible to think of holding men responsible for their deeds and thoughts before such an almighty Being?"[5] Einstein therefore spoke of the "decisive weaknesses attached to this idea . . . this concept of a personal God." His own refuge was that of the rationalist-pantheist philosopher, Spinoza (1632–1677), and with him he urged that we should think of the universe itself as God.[6] The modern British philosopher, Anthony Flew, addresses this nexus of questions and writes dismissively of "the scandalous doctrine of divine predestination."[7] Such is the drift of thought and the bequest that sophisticated opinion has made to common concern. The issue reduces, in its essence and basis, to whether we may hold securely to the existence and ordering of a personal God.[8]

In the paragraph of the Confession that begins its address to this subject with the words, "When God converts a sinner . . ." two principal points of doctrine come to prominence. It is said, first, that God's saving work "frees him [the sinner] from his natural bondage under sin, and by his grace alone enables him freely to will and to do that which is spiritually good." And second, it is said that there is still within the converted sinner "remaining corruption," as a result of which "he doth not perfectly nor only will that which is good, but doth also will that which is evil."[9] That acknowledged fact of "remaining corruption" appears at other points of the confessional statement.

In the sixth chapter of the Confession the claim appears, "This *corruption of nature*, during this life, doth remain in those that are regenerated."[10] Again, in its discussion of the doctrine of sanctification the Confession refers to the "*remaining corruption*" in the Christian believer and comments that "there abideth still some *remnants of corruption* in every part."[11] Further, in addressing the important doctrine of the perse-

5. Einstein, *Out of My Later Years*, 26–27, cited in Flew, *Western Philosophy*, 222.

6. See Flew, idem, loc. cit.

7. Ibid., 234.

8. From the side of the theologians see Luther, *Bondage of the Will*, and Edwards, *Freedom of the Will*.

9. Westminster Confession, IX, 4.

10. Ibid., VI, 5, italics added.

11. Ibid., XIII, 2 and 3, italics added.

verance of the saints reference is made to "the prevalency of *corruption remaining* in them [Christian believers]." [12] Finally, when the Confession turns to discuss the place and function of the law of God it concludes that among other aspects of the law's function it is operative in "discovering . . . the *sinful pollutions* of their [the Christians'] nature" and that it is accordingly "of use to the regenerate, to *restrain their corruptions.*" [13]

The doctrine we are at present addressing implies the following proposition: *There remains in the regenerate Christian what the Westminster Confession refers to as the "corruption of nature," but that is not to be understood as saying, and it cannot be claimed, that there remains in the Christian a "corrupt nature."* We are interested now in what is to be held as biblically consistent doctrine regarding the relation that is here contemplated between "corruption of nature" and "corrupt nature." The "corruption" remains, that is, but there does not exist within the Christian person a "corrupt nature." Differences of understanding at this point have been current in the history of evangelicalism and a clarification is called for of what is involved in the relevant debates.

The argument that follows asks whether there is in the regenerate Christian both an old corrupt nature and a new regenerate nature. Should we hold, that is to say, a "two natures theory" in our description of the regenerate Christian person? That question will be answered in the negative. We shall dissent from the suggestion proposed by the question and will conclude that the Christian person is simply a new person ("old things are passed away . . . all things are become new" [2 Cor.5:17]), and we shall emphasize the integral nature of his regenerate personhood that means he is accordingly characterized most simply and necessarily by a new nature. Our conclusion will be that the person is what his nature is. The regenerate man is a new man because he is now characterized by a new nature. Scriptural data that bear on the doctrine will be adduced. [14]

12. Westminster Confession, XVII, 3, italics added.

13. Ibid., XIX, 6, italics added.

14. Hughes comments insightfully on the text we have cited, 2 Cor. 5:17, that the aorist tense of the verb "passed away" "points back to a definite moment or event, namely, the experience of the new birth." But the perfect tense of the "become new" indicates that "the old things became and continue to be new; for the newness of God's creation is not a newness that in course of time palls and grows old and outmoded; it is a newness that is everlastingly new." Observing on God's statement in Rev. 21:4–5, "the first things are passed away . . . I make all things new," Hughes comments that the Christian "as a man-in-Christ . . . is in fact a new creation—a reborn microcosm belonging to the

We have noted that the second of two points of doctrine raised by the Confession was to the effect that the regenerate person does not always and invariably do that which is good, but that he also does that which is evil. If that conclusion is doctrinally sound (and there is adequate biblical data to demonstrate that it is), two further questions arise. First, is that apparently conflicting characterization of the converted human condition what it is because of a defect in the saving work of God of which the Confession has already spoken? Or secondly, are we to trace the causation of continuing "evil" rather than uninterrupted "good" in the converted person to a defect in the human soul? Is continuing sin, that is to say, God's fault or man's fault? Is salvation really, and in the last analysis, defective in that it fails to achieve its intended or hoped-for purpose; or is the fuller meaning of that purpose discoverable only on a deeper level of argument or revelation? The biblical data, again, are replete with answers to our questions. The divine will and purpose cannot be impugned. And to raise the suggestion of defect in the human soul is to side-track argument into a theological blind alley and a doctrinal dead end. We shall see that to do so is to contradict a central reality that must be allowed to inform our conclusion; namely, the reality of the integral nature, soul and body, of human personhood, in both its regenerate and its unregenerate state.

What, then, is at issue? Two doctrines that stand at the heart of the Reformed Christian confession throw clarifying light on the matters at hand. In the first place, a clear understanding is to be held of the meaning and effects of the regenerating work of the Holy Spirit of God in the soul of man; and second, the internal status of the soul that results from regeneration, the character and conjunction of the faculties of the soul, is to be seen as describing the true nature of the person who is now new-born in Christ.

WHAT IS REGENERATION?

We have said that our thesis requires the recognition of the reality and the existential implications of the integral nature of human personhood. What, then, is the significance for that condition of the Holy Spirit's work of regeneration to which we have just referred? It is clear from the doc-

---

eschatological macrocosm of the new heavens and the new earth—for whom the old order of things has given place to a transcendental experience in which everything is new," Hughes, *Corinthians*, 201–204.

trinal structure of the Westminster/Savoy/Baptist Confessions that our fathers of the seventeenth century spoke of regeneration in somewhat different terms from those that subsequently gained currency. They encompassed the doctrine of regeneration within what they referred to as "effectual calling."[15] That, as the Westminster Shorter Catechism refers to it, "is the work of God's Spirit, whereby, convincing us of our sin and misery, enlightening our minds in the knowledge of Christ, and renewing our wills, he doth persuade and enable us to embrace Jesus Christ, freely offered to us in the gospel."[16] Regeneration is a complex, radical, and sovereign work of the Spirit of God that turns a sinner to seek Christ in a whole-souled repentance and faith. The catechetical statement we have just inspected contemplates that work of the Holy Spirit under the fivefold headings of convincing, enlightening, renewing, persuading, and enabling. Regeneration, we have said in other places, is "that sovereign and unsolicited act of the Holy Spirit of God within the soul, whereby the faculties of the soul, the mind, heart, will, and conscience, or the intellectual, emotional, volitional, and judicial faculties, are endowed with abilities and capacities they did not previously possess, and there is created within the soul a new disposition or principle of action."[17]

Regeneration does not involve the creation of any new faculties that the individual on and in whom the Spirit's work is performed did not previously possess. Rather, as has been said, it involves the endowment of the faculties with new abilities and capacities. By the work of regeneration one is brought by an unsolicited divine intervention to a knowledge of God that was once foreign and unimaginable. With a new awareness that before could not have been contemplated or understood, the mind, the intellectual faculty that was once blinded by the god of this world, is enlightened. "For God, who commanded the light to shine out of darkness, hath shined in our hearts, to give the light of the knowledge of the glory of God in the face of Jesus Christ" (2 Cor. 4:6). The heart or the emotional faculty that was once consumed by a hatred of God (Rom. 1:30) now turns with a new desire for God to seek after him. The will or the volitional faculty is renewed and the soul that hated God and fled from every thought and suggestion and imagination of God and his law is now his willing servant.

15. See Westminster Confession, X.

16. Westminster Shorter Catechism, Question 31.

17. Vickers, *Christian Confession*, 144.

"Ye have obeyed [the volitional faculty active in its new-found freedom] from the heart [the instigation and concurrence of the emotional faculty] that form of doctrine [the determinative action of the intellectual faculty] which was delivered you" (Rom. 6:17). "Thy people," the Psalmist anticipates, "shall be willing in the day of thy power" (Ps. 110:3).

It may appear that in what has just been said in our reference to the faculties of the soul we have fallen into an old and much-discussed doctrinal difficulty that has been addressed under the heading of faculty psychology. We may clarify what is involved by reference to the well-known eighteenth-century work of Jonathan Edwards on the *Freedom of the Will*. In that work, which was designed as a demolition of Arminianism or, as Conrad Cherry puts it, "to reduce the arguments of the Arminians to absurdity,"[18] Edwards insists on and sets out to clarify the *interdependence* of the faculties of the soul as their activity culminates in an action of the will. For example, in rejecting forcibly "the Arminian notion of freedom, that the will influences, orders, and determines itself,"[19] Edwards comments that "every act of the will is some way connected with the understanding, and is as the greatest apparent good is."[20] And "It is . . . impossible for the will to choose contrary to its own . . . preponderating inclination."[21] On the conjunction of the actions of the faculties that Edwards thus envisages, Cherry contrasts Edwards' work with the rationalistic Arminianism of Charles Chauncy. Chauncy, Cherry concludes, "is a captive of the scholastic psychology which breaks human agency into *related but separate* faculties."[22] But Edwards, Cherry argues, rejects the scholastic faculty psychology because he rejects the *autonomous*, uninstructed activity of the faculties *separately considered*.

Our own argument is to the same effect. For our present argument, the soulish activity of the person is to be understood as the activity of what we shall refer to as his integral personhood. It is that integral character of human action that now engages us and which will throw its light on the understanding of the actions and the process of life of the Christian

---

18. Cherry, *Theology of Jonathan Edwards*, 160.
19. Edwards, *Freedom of the Will*, 45.
20. Ibid., 86.
21. Ibid., 73.
22. Cherry, op. cit., 167, italics added.

believer.[23] We avoid the difficulties of the "scholastic faculty psychology" because we hold, in a manner not inconsistent with that of Edwards, not to the *separate and independent* capacities and actions of the faculties, but to the *interdependence* that inevitably exists between them, and to the jointness of their determination of action, as that is attributable to the human individual in his or her integral personhood.

REGENERATE PERSONHOOD

Our argument to this point has prepared the way for a direct consideration of what we have observed the Westminster Confession to state regarding the capacities and actions of the person who is now regenerate in Christ. He is now free to will and act in obedience to the mandated will of God. But he is also capable of evil, and while he does the "good," he also does the "evil" of which the Confession has spoken in several places. What, now, are we to understand as the meaning of what is involved on those dimensions of the Christian life? How, to take up a motif we have just referred to, does the integral nature of individual personhood bear on our answer to the question?

An efficient point of entry to answering our questions is provided by the statement in Romans 6:6 that "our old man is crucified with [Christ]." The text at that point goes on to indicate and to emphasize the purpose or objective that is in view in what is there described as the death of the old man. The purpose is, as the text states it, "that the body of sin might be destroyed." Now in the history of commentary there has been a divergence of opinion, to which we shall return, as to the meaning in that context of "the body of sin." But our questions require us to be clear, first, as to the meaning of the "old man" that is "crucified with Christ." The "old man" is the Adamic man. It is the Adamic man as that was characterized after, and as a result of, the fall. That man, it is well known and well argued in the Reformed expression of the Christian faith, is the man who is "dead in trespasses and sins" (Eph. 2:1). It is the man who, as the Confession has it in the context we are examining, is in a state of "natural bondage under

---

23. It is of interest that Edwards, in his characterization of the "two faculties of the soul," follows John Calvin who observes that "the human soul consists of two faculties, understanding and will" (*Institutes,* vol. 1, 194). But Edwards, as does Calvin, accords significant action to the affective capacity or faculty of the soul and he appears to take account of the wider faculty designation we have adopted. In his *Charity and Its Fruits,* 58, Edwards observes that "a man has a heart, and an understanding, and a will."

sin." It cannot yet be said of him that he has been "delivered from the power of darkness and translated into the kingdom of [God's] dear Son" (Col. 1:13). He has not yet been "translated into the state of grace" to which the Confession refers.[24] But we are concerned at this point to understand what is to be said of the man after that translation has taken place. He is "crucified with Christ." The "body of sin" has been destroyed. And yet the new man in Christ is characterized by "remaining corruption."

What, then, is to be understood as "the body of sin?" As we observed in a different context in the preceding chapter, many commentators have understood the reference here to be to the "mass of sin" that supposedly characterizes the man. That is essentially the view of no less an exegete than John Calvin, who says that "*The body of sin . . .* does not mean flesh and bones, but the corrupted mass; for man, left to his own nature, is a mass made up of sin."[25] Further instances of that line of exposition are referred to in John Murray's commentary on the text. But there is good reason to conclude that the reference here in the word "body" is to our actual physical body. Lloyd-Jones takes that position in his sermonic commentary.[26] John Murray also draws attention to the usages in the Pauline vocabulary of the "body" as referring to the physical, mortal body and concludes that in the present instance the "body of sin" means "the body as conditioned and controlled by sin."[27] Of course, the physical body is not yet dead, as the fact that you are reading this confirms. What is being said, therefore, is that the purpose of the death of the old man is that *the whole man has thereby made a definitive breach with sin* and that, moreover, that breach "should be conceived of as drawing within its scope the body as well as the spirit of the believer."[28]

That in itself, as Murray has stated it, should strike us as a remarkable conclusion. The grasp of it is assisted by the recognition of the nature of the human person as we have referred previously to the individual in his integral personhood. For in characterizing the being and nature of man we do not say that he *has* a body and that he *has* a soul. If we were to say that we would be speaking in a most ungainly fashion of a triad: first, the

24. Westminster Confession, IX, 4.

25. John Calvin, Commentary ad loc. cit.

26. Lloyd-Jones, *Romans . . . Chapter 6*, 72.

27. Murray, *Romans*, vol. 1, 220.

28. Ibid., 221.

man himself, secondly the body he is said to possess, and third the soul he possesses. But we say, rather, not that man *has* a body and a soul, but that he *is* body and soul. We may ask, then, what is to be said of man in his bodily aspect, and what is to be said of him in his soulish aspect, as those aspects are in view in his regenerate or unregenerate state respectively? As to the present question of the "body of sin," we conclude with Murray that "the body is an integral part of personality,"[29] or, to employ again our alternative nomenclature, the body is an aspect of man's integral person- hood. We shall observe in a moment other theological references to the same conception. But the conclusion to be held is that by reason of the death of the old man, his "crucifixion with Christ," the man in his bodily aspect is no longer "conditioned and controlled by sin," as in his soulish aspect he is no longer conditioned and controlled by sin. John Murray again has concluded to the same effect.[30] In most straightforward terms, "the body of sin is destroyed" in the death of the "old man" because, as the resulting objective comes to effect, the body is no longer conditioned and controlled by sin. That is the point of doctrine that is to be cognized and whose existential implications are to be worked out.

It should be inserted at this point that Lloyd-Jones, in his otherwise very valuable commentary, has concluded in this entire connection that while, as has been noted, he understands the "body of sin" to have refer- ence to the physical, mortal body, he goes on to say that the fuller refer- ence of "the body of sin" is to "sin as it dwells in our present embodied condition."[31] In doing so he effectively aligns with those who, as men- tioned earlier, regard the "body of sin" as a mass of corruption. That, as already noted, follows Calvin. Further, Lloyd-Jones expands his argument from the point under review to conclude that the "body of sin" means "the old nature."[32] That, therefore, affords a prominent instance of what we contemplated earlier as a "two natures" theory of the being of man. For Lloyd-Jones the "old man" is dead, having been crucified with Christ as Romans 6:6 declares, but the "old nature" still exists and is alive in the re- generate person. Lloyd-Jones sums up by saying, "my carnal, sinful nature

29. Murray, idem.
30. Idem.
31. Lloyd-Jones, op. cit., 72.
32. Ibid., 79.

... is still here, but the old man has gone, he has been crucified."[33] Man is, in that scheme of things, a most interesting bifurcation or dichotomy. He is one new man. But he is a man with two natures, one old and one new. Our argument dissents from that doctrinal conclusion.

We note at this point a closely related apostolic statement that appears in Galatians 5:24: "They that are Christ's have crucified the flesh . . ." The question arises of when the crucifixion envisaged in that text is to be understood as having taken place. We note the aorist tense of the verb "crucified," and we reflect on the point in time to which, as a result, the text refers. We see every reason to believe that the time-date in view is nothing other than that of the believer's participation in the death of Christ, in the sense in which Romans 6:6 has already explained that. The one who is in Christ, as the Galatians text says, understands that the flesh, meaning by that all that is meant by the thought-forms and behavior-norms of the world-system as antithetical to the holiness of God, was crucified when Christ died and conveyed the benefits of his death to his elect people. The "crucifixion of the flesh" referred to in the Galatian letter does not, for example, have to do with a stage or point in the Christian believer's progress in sanctification. The death contemplated is referable to the point of the believer's entry to the state of justification as that is suspended on the death of Christ.

But such an understanding of the text may sit ill, it may be feared, with the apostle's further argument in the same chapter of the Galatian letter that "the flesh lusteth against the Spirit, and the Spirit against the flesh" (Gal. 5:17). No contradiction, however, exists. For the latter context takes up precisely what is to be said about the question of sin in the regenerate person, and it aligns, therefore, with the statement of the Confession with which we started, namely that the regenerate person is capable of both good and evil. A resolution of this question will follow a fuller explanation of the two natures theory.

THE "TWO NATURES" THEORY

The doctrine from which we are now dissenting was given explicit and influential currency by the translation of the New International Version of the Scriptures. Consistent with its tendency to translate the word "flesh" as "sinful nature," that version refers at Romans 8:5, for example, to "those who live according to the sinful nature . . ." The NIV translation continues

33. Lloyd-Jones, op. cit. 63.

that usage in the following verses in the same chapter of the letter to the Romans. But the doctrine itself has an extensive parentage and usage. To see its implications more clearly, let us draw together now the threads of our argument so far.

For the regenerate believer, who is now joined to Christ, it is properly said that "the old man has been crucified with Christ." When Christ died, that is to say, the elect sinner died. He was, and is, identified with Christ in all that Christ did in the discharge of his redemptive-messianic assignment. "Buried with him," the text says (Rom. 6:4), "also risen with him" (Col. 2:12), and therefore "when Christ, who is our life, shall appear, then shall ye also appear with him in glory" (Col. 3:4). By reason of the crucifixion of the old man the body of sin is destroyed, meaning, as has been said, that *a definitive breach with sin has been made* and that the individual, in both his bodily and his soulish aspects, is no longer conditioned and controlled by sin. The new man in Christ is a new man in every respect that pertains to his relations with God, his journey in this life, and his prospects for the life to come. The old has definitively passed away. The individual person has been translated into an entirely new realm of being and behavior. But while that is so, the new man in Christ commits sin. That is the blunt reality, and our enquiry now is how that apparent conflict and contradiction is to be explained. Does the explanation lie in the fact that the regenerate person possesses two natures, one old and one new? If that were so, the explanation of sin could be simply stated by saying that it is never the new nature that sins. It is always the old nature, or as the NIV translation says, the "sinful nature," that sins. But the reality is that it is not one of a dual of natures that sins. When one sins it is the person who sins. And the person in the act and conduct of sin is responsible, alarmingly responsible, for his sin. That is the dilemma of the two natures theory. That, of course, is saying again from another perspective that the individual person is one indivisible personality, or, to employ alternative terminology again, he is to be characterized as one, and to be regarded as one, integral personhood.

We do not therefore say only or simply that the regenerate person has a new nature. We say, rather, that by reason of the regenerating work of the Spirit of God in the soul the person himself is "new" by virtue of the characteristics of nature that now describe him. Because of what we have just recalled as the integral nature of the individual in his personhood, and because the characteristics of nature that now describe him are what they are because the Holy Spirit has endowed him with them, it is not a matter of possessing both an "old" and a "new" nature. The person in Christ is what he is simply because the characteristics of nature that now describe him are what they are. Again the man is what his nature is. The "nature" is what describes the man.

The doctrine from which we are dissenting is traceable to a teaching that was prominent in Plymouth Brethren circles in the mid-nineteenth century and which was given further prominence in the Scofield Bible. Scofield has argued that "The Scriptures teach that every regenerate person is the possessor of two natures: one, received by natural birth, which is wholly and hopelessly bad; and a new nature, received through the new birth, which is the nature of God Himself, and therefore wholly good .... The believer ... while still having his old nature, unchanged and unchangeable, has received a new nature which 'after God is created in righteousness and true holiness.'"[34] And in its comment on the text of Romans 7:15 the *Scofield Reference Bible* (1909 edition) states that "The apostle personifies the strife of the two natures in the believer, the old or Adamic nature, and the divine nature received through the new birth."[35]

Robert Dabney, a nineteenth-century theologian who was influential in the southern American states, has examined the two natures theory at length.[36] Dabney states that "we challenge them [the two natures theorists] to produce a text from the New Testament where it is said that regeneration is the implantation of a 'new *nature*' beside the old; or that the renewed man has two hostile '*natures*,' or any such language .... [Paul] teaches that the renewed man (one man and one nature still) is imperfect, having two principles of volition mixed in the motives even of the same acts; but he does not teach that he has become 'two men,' or has 'two natures' in him."[37] Again, "the bible is still further from saying that the renewed man has two '*natures*.' For then he would be two men, unless every conversion is a miracle of hypostatic union, like Christ's incarnation."[38]

34. Scofield, *Rightly Dividing the Word of Truth*, 44–49, cited in Martin, *Accuracy of Translation*, 35–36.

35. Cited in Martin, op. cit., 36. See the fuller discussion in Martin, op. cit., 32ff.

36. Dabney, "Theology of the Plymouth Brethren," reprinted in Dabney, *Discussions*, vol. 1, 169–228.

37. Dabney, op. cit., 192–93.

38. Ibid., 194.

Dabney is here taking up the same notion as we have advanced under the heading of the regenerate individual's integral personhood. John Murray takes a very similar stance when he says, as we have already noted, that "the body is an integral part of personality."[39] Murray further observes in a different context that "It is no more feasible to call the believer a new man and an old man, than it is to call him a regenerate man and an unregenerate."[40] And Murray continues, indicating at the same time the nature of the conclusion we shall reach regarding the fact of sin in the life of the Christian believer: "The believer is a new man, a new creation, but he is a new man not yet made perfect. Sin dwells in him still, and he still commits sin. He is necessarily the subject of progressive renewal . . . But this *progressive* renewal is not represented as the putting off of the old man and the putting on of the new, nor is it to be conceived of as the progressive crucifixion of the old man."[41] Murray, who has observed that "it is a mistake to think of the believer as both an old man and new man or as having in him both the old man and the new man, the latter in view of regeneration and the former because of remaining corruption,"[42] would certainly not agree with the view of Abraham Kuyper that "God's child remains the old man's grave-digger until the hour of his own departure."[43]

Dabney further clarifies the argument we are making that the regenerate person is not the possessor of two natures in his statement that such a claim "contradicts the consciousness of every Christian, even the most unlearned; for just as surely as he has one consciousness, he knows that he is one indivisible personality, and that he is one agent and has *only one will*, swayed indeed by mixed and diverse motives."[44] That "mixture of motivations" that describes the possibility of sin in the life of the Christian will engage us again. But Dabney's fuller discussion of its significance is worthy of brief summary at this point. He comments that "While the power which regenerates and sanctifies must ever be partly incomprehensible to us, the comprehension of the effect is so far easy, that the new birth *reverses* the moral *habitus* [disposition] of the believer's will, prevalently,

---

39. Murray, *Romans*, vol. 1, 221.
40. Murray, *Principles of Conduct*, 218.
41. Ibid., 219.
42. Murray, *Romans*, vol. 1, 219–220.
43. Quoted in Lloyd-Jones, op. cit., 79.
44. Dabney, op. cit., 196.

but not at first absolutely, and that the work of progressive sanctification carries on this change, thus omnipotently begun, towards that absolute completeness which we must possess on entering heaven. In the carnal state, the *habitus* of the sinner's will is absolutely and exclusively god-less. In the regenerate state it is prevalently but not completely godly. In the glorified state it is absolutely and exclusively godly. This statement implies that the believer's motives, in the militant state, are complex; and that while the subjective motives usually dominant are godly, yet there is a mixture of carnal motives, no longer dominant . . . . And this complex of subjective motives, of which one part may be morally diverse from another, may result in a single act of volition—the volition strictly *one*, while the motives prompting it are mingled."[45]

THE REMAINING CORRUPTION

We now have in place what is necessary to answer the question with which we began. What is to be said of the claim of the Westminster Confession that "When God converts a sinner, and translates him into the state of grace . . . by reason of his remaining corruption, he . . . does also that which is evil"? We are concerned, then, with the troubling fact and problem of sin in the life of the believer. Our answer is implicit, and even to some extent explicit, in what we have already said. When it is said that the regenerate person is a new person, characterized by a wholly different nature from what previously described him, we nevertheless acknowledge that that person sins. How, then, is that to be explained? Because it is the person who sins, it is the person who is responsible for the sin. So our doctrine does not in any way minimize the reality or the seriousness of sin. Rather, it emphasizes it.

The question resolves to that of the meaning of indwelling sin in the life of the believer, as Paul, for example, addresses it in that remarkable paragraph in the seventh chapter of his letter to the Romans.[46] Or to put the matter in terms similar to those we have already employed, we say

45. Dabney, op. cit., 196–97.

46. It is well known that an extensive literature exists regarding the identity of the man in Romans 7. We hold to what is essentially a consistently-held Reformed tradition that Paul is describing there the struggle of the regenerate person against indwelling sin. For a dissent from that see Lloyd-Jones' commentary on loc. cit. in *Romans . . . Chapters 7:1–8:4*, and the work of Ridderbos in *Paul*, 126ff. The dissent is continued in Reymond, *New Systematic Theology*, 1127.

that there remains in the believer a measure, greater or less, of indwelling sin, but that it is not to be said that he has a sinful nature. All we have said regarding the integral nature of personhood and the singularity of individual consciousness stands in the way of such a conclusion. We hold that it is the nature of the man that describes the man. The man is what his nature is. And because, by the regenerating grace of God, the man's nature is new, he is a new man. It is not necessary at this point to repeat our preceding argument at length to recall, as Murray, for example, has stated it, that as a result of the believer's death with Christ it is now to be said that in his bodily aspect, as in his aspect of soul, he is *no longer conditioned and controlled by sin*. The faculties of soul have been endowed with new abilities. But the faculties have not yet been made perfect in holiness. The believer lives in an environment that is in itself and in essence sinful. And in that environment, as he progresses in his gradual conformity to the likeness of Christ to which he is called, the believer can and does fall into sin for essentially two reasons. The recognition of those reasons points to the resolution of whatever tension might be introduced by the twofold statements of the Westminster Confession with which we began.

In the first place, the faculties of soul that jointly determine individual action in the way we have seen are still in this world in a state of lesser or greater degrees of development towards the perfection that they will at last enjoy. They are accordingly still capable of being deceived by sin, by the allurements of the world, and by the subtleties of the devil and his angels. The faculties have been renewed in principle and to progressive degrees in fact, but their transformation to the image of the holiness of God has not yet been perfected.

Secondly, we recall now that the Holy Spirit's act of regeneration involves not only the renewal of endowments of the faculties of the person, but also the implantation within the soul of a new disposition or principle of action. In that context we recall Dabney's conclusion that there exists within the believer a "mixture of motives" which together determine the action of will of the individual. There is in the regenerate individual, as Dabney put it, a new *habitus* or, as we have labeled it, principle of action. And that new principle has displaced the erstwhile hegemony of the old *habitus* of the previously existing sinful nature. The new principle, recognizing again the apostolic claims of indwelling sin, does not yet prevail completely, though the prevalency of the old principle of action is, in the course of the believer's sanctification, progressively diminished.

But what, more precisely, is to be understood as the old *habitus* or principle of action that can and does at times pull the believer into occasions of sin? It is simply that old habits, old preferences, and old alignments can and do from time to time raise their head and remind the believer of the old pleasures of sin. For that reason, sin in the life of the believer is explained, first, by the pressures and temptations to sin that come from outside of himself; and secondly, by the very capacity to respond to that by the habits of earlier life whose ingrained residence in the soul is being progressively displaced.

But the Scriptural data require us to state that last point as clearly as possible. As to the proper characterization of sin in the life of the believer, the apostle James has clarified for us that "every man is tempted, when he is drawn away of his own lust, and enticed" (Jas. 1:14). What are we to say of what James has referred to as that remaining "lust" in the renewed person? It is well known that the Roman Catholic church, consistently with the deliverances of the Council of Trent, insists that the lust we have in view, or what it refers to as concupiscence, is not in itself sinful, though it may well lead to sin.[47] But that doctrinal claim has been rigorously denied by the Reformed theology from which the Tridentine Council dissented. The concupiscence, the remaining lust, in the renewed person is itself sinful, as the Westminster/Savoy/Baptist doctrine on the point maintains: "This corruption of nature . . . *itself*, and all the motions thereof, are truly and properly sin."[48] What is relevant, then, is that what Dabney has referred to as the "old *habitus*," the old principle of action, or the old disposition from which the Christian believer is not yet wholly free, is itself sinful and that it is capable of rising and coming to expression in the entertainment of sin.

We can put that differently in the language of the seventeenth-century Puritan theologian, John Owen. In his treatise, *A Discourse Concerning the Holy Spirit*, Owen addresses the reality of sin in the life of the truly regenerate person. "One thing yet remains to be cleared," Owen says, "that there may be no mistake in this matter; and this is, that in those who are constantly inclined and disposed unto all the acts of a heavenly, spiritual life, there are yet remaining contrary dispositions and inclinations also. There are yet in them inclinations and dispositions to sin, *proceeding from the remainders*

---

47. See Cunningham, *Historical Theology*, vol. 1, 528–42.
48. Westminster Confession, VI, 5, italics added.

of a contrary habitual principle. . . . This yet continueth in them, inclining them unto evil and all that is so, according to the power and efficacy that is remaining unto it in various degrees. . . . There are in the same mind, will, and affections, namely, of a person regenerate, contrary habits and inclinations, continually opposing one another, and acting adversely about the same objects and ends."[49] Owen's argument is reflected in that of Dabney. And what Owen refers to as the "contrary habitual principle" is again a reference to what is described in the Scriptures as indwelling sin. "This," Owen says by way of conclusion, "the Scripture calls . . . the 'sin that dwelleth in us.'"[50]

Sinclair Ferguson, in his *John Owen on the Christian Life*, comments on Owen's acknowledgment that "there are 'contrary inclinations and dispositions' [in the regenerate person] but these proceed from the '*remainders* of a contrary habitual principle' described in the Scriptures as the flesh or indwelling sin."[51] Ferguson continues in his interpretation of Owen (loc. cit.), and, effectively confirming the theses we have advanced in the foregoing, he writes: "Hence conflict arises: This is not between the 'distinct faculties of the soul itself' as in the natural man, but between contrary habits and inclinations in the *same* mind, will and affections in the believer. That is, the conflict lies, not between the faculties, but 'in the same faculties'. To this the apostle Paul refers in Galatians 5:17."[52]

But what are we to say of the true believer's response to the realization of the meaning of such occasions of sin in his life? The answer to that question can be stated briefly at this point as threefold. First, Paul, in the sixth chapter of his letter to the Romans from which we have already quoted, states the imperative that lies upon the Christian believer by saying "Reckon ye also yourselves to be dead indeed unto sin, but alive unto God through Jesus Christ our Lord" (Rom. 6:11). It is not that reckoning oneself dead to sin makes one dead to sin. Rather, Paul's injunction follows from the logic of his preceding argument and states that because the old man has been crucified with Christ the new man-in-Christ is now dead to sin. Paul is saying that we must realize the profound reality of that fact situation and allow the tenor of our lives to be determined by it. Sin,

---

49. Owen, *Pneumatologia*, in *Works*, vol. 3, 488, italics added.

50. Idem.

51. Ferguson, *John Owen on the Christian Life*, 64.

52. Ibid., 64–65.

Paul is saying, no longer has anything to do with the Christian, and why, therefore, should the Christian have anything to do with sin?

Second, the true believer is to realize that sin no longer has dominion over him. He may and he does fall into occasions of sin, but because he has been translated definitively from the realm of sin, he is no longer subject to its damning imperatives. The Christian has been transferred by the grace of God from an old realm, as John Murray has put it, of sin, condemnation, and death to a realm of righteousness, justification, and life.[53] It is because of that definitive transference that the apostle can say, "old things are passed away; behold, all things are become new" (2 Cor. 5:17).

Third, the believer is to know, on the grounds of the eternal veracity of God who has saved his people in fulfillment of the covenant he made with his elect in Christ, that "he which hath begun a good work in you will perform it until the day of Jesus Christ" (Phil. 1:6). The doctrine of the "perseverance of the saints," which the Westminster Confession goes on to consider beyond the chapter we have examined,[54] makes it clear, not only that the eternal security of the believer has been firmly established, but that it is by the grace of God that the inheritance in the eternal kingdom of Christ that has been promised to the believer has been guaranteed (Heb. 9:15). Notwithstanding the occasions of sin in this life that we have inspected, notwithstanding what may result, as the Confession states it, from "the prevalency of corruption remaining in them," the true believers "shall be kept by the power of God through faith unto salvation" (1 Pet. 1:5). We shall return to that important point.

All that being said, a final question may arise from the very definition and explanation we have given of the Holy Spirit's act of regeneration in the soul of an individual. We have said that regeneration involves the endowment of the faculties of the soul with new abilities and capacities they did not previously possess. But the faculties themselves, we have said, are the same faculties as they have always been. The individual in what we have termed his integral personhood is the same person. The faculties are now, however, differently endowed. That being so, we have brought to emphasis the fact that, as a result, the person who is the beneficiary of that act of regeneration is a "new" person. We have said also that the "nature" of the individual describes the "person," or that the person is what his

53. Murray, *Romans*, 179.
54. See Westminster Confession, XVII.

nature is. And the thrust of the Scriptural data warrant our saying that the person who is now new in nature is a new person. But a final question may follow. How can it properly be said that the regenerate person is the "same" person he was before, but that in respects to be carefully understood he is now a "new" person? How can it be said that he is the same, and yet he is new?

In the light of that question let us cast our minds back to Adam and his fall. The fall was an ethical lapse. By that we mean that on the level of action and behavior Adam did what he ought not to have done. He ate the forbidden fruit. The result and the significance it has for all those descending from him by ordinary generation are well-known. They lie at the very base of what we understand as the necessity and the divine *modus operandi* of redemption. By saying that the fall was an ethical lapse, we mean that it did not cause or imply any change in Adam's metaphysical (ontological) state. It did not change him, that is to say, into a being other than he was before. When we say, then, that the fall was an ethical, not a metaphysical, lapse, (or that it was ethical, not ontic) we are driving home two things: first the continuity of being, and secondly the continuity of responsibility and accountability, of Adam.

At this point we leave unsaid all that we have seen follows from the bequest to us of Adam's fall. We look now at man as the same metaphysical (ontological) being or entity that he always was. That being so, what regeneration does to a person is again not to cause or imply any metaphysical change or change in status of being. That is why the person is the "same" person. Another way of conceiving of that "sameness" is to recall our statement that the human faculties after the fall are the same faculties; they are the same faculties (given the continuity of integral and responsible personhood), but they do not, after the fall, possess the same abilities as they did in Adam's pristine state. But then the question arises: If regeneration does not cause a metaphysical change (or change in essential being), what does it do? Leaving aside all that we have already said it does in the matter of conveying new endowments to the soul, let us look for a moment at the respect in which it accomplishes a reversal of Adam's primeval movement from holiness to curse. Adam's fall was ethical, we say, not metaphysical. So, to focus our thought on the reversal that is involved in regeneration, are we to say that regeneration is again ethical, and not metaphysical?

There is an important element of truth in that suggestion. But though we may follow that line of thought, we may say more precisely that regeneration has that effect on and in the soulish aspect of the person that reverses his ethical capacity and potential. Then, regeneration being in itself the beginning of sanctification, that renewal of ethical capacity enables the person to exhibit increasingly the fruits of the actual ethical reversal that regeneration accomplishes. In that sense, the person is the "same" person as to his responsible and accountable being (metaphysically), but a "new" person as to his ability and capacity to walk in righteousness before God (ethically) and not to sin as Adam did.

One more thing, however, is to be said. While we hold to the fact that as to the essence and being of the person regeneration does not imply a metaphysical change, we do say that the person who is the beneficiary of it, the person in what we have referred to as his integral personhood, has been raised to a new state of existence. That new state is described by saying that now he is joined to Christ in an actual and indissoluble union. That existential element of union with Christ carries with it, of course, vast theological and salvific significance, a significance that is beyond our present objectives to examine further at this time. We shall return to the question of the believer's union with Christ in a later chapter. But that union is in itself an element of the "newness" of the person that is involved. It does not destroy or change the person's created being (metaphysics), personhood, and responsibility. But it raises that same state of being to a new higher level of existence that now has eternal properties inherent in it.

CONCLUSION

Our conclusion can be briefly stated without any repetition of the argument. "Remaining corruption" does work within the believer, as the seventeenth-century Confessions state, but it cannot be said that the believer has a "corrupt nature." He is a *new* nature, a *new* man in Christ Jesus, a *new* person, and that "newness" is to determine his outlook, his conduct, and his prospects in this life in anticipation of the reward of inheritance that is reserved in heaven for him.

But to state our conclusion in that form raises a complex of biblical doctrines we must note briefly but on which we cannot enter at length at this late stage. We have said, and the Scriptures clearly maintain the claim, that by the sovereign act of the omniscient, omnipotent God certain sinners, those whom God chose in his gracious predestinating decree before the foundation of the world, have been born again to a newness of life. We have contemplated the connotation of that "newness" and its implications, and we have endeavored to rebut certain misconceptions regarding it. But the question has been asked frequently in the history of doctrine whether that "newness" is, or is not, reversible. The Arminians have made great play on particularly that question. They have widely asserted that a true believer in Christ may fall away from the grace of God that first brought him into a state of salvation and be eternally lost. The Arminian doctrine amounts to the suggestion that one who has been made regenerate can, by reason of his supposed free will and personal sovereignty, become again unregenerate. The doctrine that calls for at least minimal notice is therefore what has been explored under the heading of the perseverance of the saints. At this point, and in the light of all that has been said, we make only two comments regarding it.

First, we note what the doctrine of the perseverance of the saints does *not* mean or imply. It does *not* mean that after regeneration and faith has been imparted to an individual he or she will be "admitted, *as a matter of course*, to heaven, without any regard to the moral history of the intervening period."[55] Our conception of "newness" that turns on the regenerating grace of God involves the claim that in all of his purposes with relation to the redemption and the eternal security of his elect, God has ordained all of the means as well as the ends. That implies that the perseverance of the saints takes up and establishes more than the destiny, or the end, or the inheritance that is aimed at. What is involved in the perseverance of the saints is their perseverance in the life and progress of holiness to which they have been called and established in Christ. Those whom Christ redeemed will, by reason of God's renewing grace that is without repentance on his part, be kept by his Spirit in the "newness" in which they have been established.

Secondly, what is finally at issue, and what follows from our argument, is that the perseverance we are speaking of is not—and this is the point that calls for clear emphasis—is not the perseverance of the sinner considered in and of himself in his state of original nature or in, as we may properly put it, his isolated or detached personhood. For at this point

---

55. See Cunningham, *Historical Theology*, vol. 2, 495, italics added.

the very nature of regenerate personhood must come again to prominent recognition. What we are speaking of is the perseverance of the person who is joined to Christ. It is by reason of the existential union with Christ, that vital and indissoluble union that the grace of regeneration establishes, that the new-born person perseveres in both the life of progressive holiness and the attainment of the end to which it indefectibly leads. The true believer perseveres because his position is such that it can only be said "I live; yet not I, but Christ liveth in me; and the life which I now live in the flesh I live by the faith of the Son of God, who loved me, and gave himself for me" (Gal. 2:20).

May that, by the grace of God, be the conscious awareness that motivates our life and actions until the end. God grant that we may each, in the various vicissitudes and life-journeys that God has marked out for us, live with calm contentment and faithful obedience to him in the light of what we have now realized to be our true state and condition.

6

The Light of His Countenance

IN THE HISTORY OF confessing Christianity no question has presented itself more acutely to the reflective mind than that of the relation between believing faith and the competence and function of human reason and its legitimacy in the Christian life. Indeed, the cleavage on the one hand, or the concurrence on the other, between reason and faith raised their complex issues at our first parents' fall that cast us all down into sin. For there the challenge to Adam was whether he would believe what God his Maker had stated to him as the condition of continued bliss and eternal life, or whether, as all too clearly and all too quickly became the case, he would make that false assertion of autonomy that attempted to raise his reasoning capacity beyond its created range and prerogatives. Presented with both the word of God and the word of the devil, Adam stated to himself that he would not believe either the one or the other. He himself would be the arbiter of appropriate belief and action. That was the genesis of the damning entrance of sin. Not the command and the caution of God, and not the contrivance of Satan, would determine his deciding action. In the supposed autonomy of his self-conscious personhood Adam insisted that on all levels of being, knowing, and behavior he was competent to make whatever decisions he himself knew were for his own ultimate good. There, in a single climactic and all-determining act, the false assumptions of metaphysical, epistemological, and ethical autonomy entered into human life and its prospects. That, we shall see, has continuing implications for the Christian life and for the proper understanding of what sin in the Christian life is and means.

The first thing to be said of sin is that it is the state to which we were reduced by Adam's fall. Sin, as the catechism sees it in its ethical import, is "any want of conformity unto, or transgression of, the law of

God,"[1] reflecting the statement of the apostle John that "sin is the transgression of the law" (1 John 3:4). We can say, further, that sin is the repudiation of covenantal obligations. In its various aspects it is that action, in thought, word, or deed, that outrages or offends the holiness of God. It is the creature's self-direction, or the love of self coming to ascendancy and replacing the love of God. But our immediate concern is to investigate the significance of the fact that sin comes to expression in the false assumption and assertion of human autonomy against God. The sin of falsely assumed autonomy was that by which Satan fell. When it is said that he "abode not in the truth . . . for he is a liar, and the father of it" (John 8:44), his first lie that cast him from heaven was the claim that he had a right to be equal with God, to be his own god. It is precisely that claim to which he seduced our first parents. A preliminary definition of the essence and scope of the assumptions of autonomy is therefore necessary.[2]

First, the assumption of *metaphysical autonomy* implies the assertion, and it implies all that is involved in action consistent with that assertion, that man is not the creature of a Creator-God. Adam, of course, knew that he had come from the hands of God. But now his assumption of autonomy meant that he was prepared to believe that whatever his origin might have been it was not now relevant to his continued existence and to whatever he might do or achieve in his life. In one of the pregnant aspects of its meaning, the import of Adam's sin is that he therein effectively denied his creaturehood. Though he was established in pristine covenantal relation with God his Maker, and though there was provided for him in the tree of life the sacramental confirmation of God's promise of beatitude on the condition of his obedience, our first parent claimed that as to the matter of being he was self-sufficiently and securely separate from God. He claimed, therefore, that he was competent to repudiate what had been conveyed to him as his covenantal obligation to God. Sin finds its deepest root and cause and character in precisely that fact. And therein it comes to its truest expression and most damning import. Sin is the repudiation of covenantal obligations. Ever since our first parents' fall, that primeval assertion of autonomy has cast its shadow and has vitiated apostate thought through the long journey of human understanding. It has determined

1. Westminster Shorter Catechism, Question 14.

2. See the reference to "the idea of human ultimacy or autonomy" and "the idea of the autonomous man" in Van Til, *Defense of the Faith*, 140, and passim, and the same author's *Christian Theory of Knowledge*, passim.

and side-tracked the claims of modern thought, from the beginning of modern philosophy in Descartes in the seventeenth century, through the eighteenth-century Enlightenment and its culmination in Kant, the positivism that followed and impregnated thought in all academic disciplines, on to twentieth-century existentialism and now the death of God and the death of man in contemporary postmodernism. Human thought and imagination became pointedly anthropocentric.

Second, the assumption of *epistemological autonomy*, or what transpires on the level of the possibility and validity of knowledge, implies that man who is now the sinner concludes that he is not subject to God-established laws of being and God-created laws of function and operation in reality external to the Godhead. Reality exists, it is imagined, in a sea of randomness and chance, and facts are "brute" in the Kantian sense that they are unrelated, exist without interpretive context, and are ultimately irrational. The facts, that is, are not *pre*interpreted by a divine mind and therefore available for *re*interpretation by the human mind, and man the knower is himself inextricable in the web of randomness his thought-forms have conjured. The criteria of knowledge, the criteria of truth and rightness, are not in any sense God-established. In all aspects of his epistemic capacity, his capacity for knowing, man is autonomously capable and free to discover his criteria within himself, to excogitate them from within his own internal self-consciousness, or to take them from his social and cultural environment. Metaphysically and epistemically man is now free from all and any external constraint and determining contexts. That is the measure of his assumptions of autonomy.

Third, it follows that because he is, as is supposed, autonomously free from God as to his being and his knowing, man is assumedly free also from God-established laws of conduct and behavior. That is his assumption of *ethical autonomy*. For being is prior to knowing and behavior. Ontology is prior to epistemology and ethics. On the level of ethics, he is again autonomously free to set his own criteria of action, as he had set his criteria of belief. Again, the criteria of right and wrong behavior in life are autonomously determined, or they are discoverable within the complex of the social and cultural milieu in which man finds himself. He is himself, as he supposes and as is implied by his own assumptions, nothing more than a chance phenomenon floating randomly on a boundless sea of indeterminateness. Man is therefore, it is now falsely assumed, neither responsible nor accountable to any being, criterion, or rule or canon external to himself. But the reality is that in his claims of autonomy he has made himself the slave of Satan and sin. He is the dupe of the devil. He is the compliant subject of the "strong man armed [that] keepeth his palace [and] his goods . . . in peace" (Luke 11:21). As our Lord stated to the remonstrating Jews on a memorable occasion, "Whosoever committeth sin is the servant [slave] of sin" (John 8:34). Man's blinded vaunt of freedom has landed him in an inextricable slavery; inextricable, that is, unless the sovereign grace of God should intervene in saving rescue and relief.

The words that caption this chapter cast their light on the sinner's resulting relation to God. In short, by virtue of what characterizes his chosen position and his claims as they have been described in what we have said, God has withdrawn from man "the light of his countenance," the comforting conviction of his presence and the assurance of his covenantal favor. The fuller declaration of the Scriptures to that effect, adequately justifying the statement of the Westminster/Savoy/Baptist confessions in the loci we have indicated, are so well-known as not to require detailed acknowledgment. The disease of sin and the divine remedy are patent on the surface of the Scriptural text. Suffice it to say that "the god of this world hath blinded the mind," and that the only source of rescue and relief is in the fact that "God, who commanded the light to shine out of darkness, hath shined in our hearts, to give the light of the knowledge of the glory of God in the face of Jesus Christ" (2 Cor. 4:4–6).

But the confessional statement to which we have referred probes beyond the truth of ultimate causation that we have inspected to this point. God has withdrawn "the light of his countenance" from man the sinner by reason of the sinner's deliberate sin. That is by now unarguable. But we shall see in what follows that God can and does withdraw the light of his countenance from the true Christian believer. In that connection two things can be said by way of anticipation. First, God the Holy Spirit who now lives in and with the Christian believer does not and will not withdraw his presence from that person. The truth of that statement is again adequately established by Scriptural data. But second, while God does not withdraw his presence from his new-born child, he may, and he does as occasion warrants, withdraw the awareness, the consciousness, and the heart-warming sensibility of that presence. It is on that loss of awareness and consciousness, not the loss of God's presence itself, that our Puritan fathers were eloquent. John Owen, for example, speaks strongly to the point. "To have peace with God, to have strength to walk before God, is the sum of the great promises of the covenant of grace. . . . Without them in some comfortable measure, to live is to die. What good will our lives do us if we see not the face of God sometimes in peace? . . . What peace, I pray, is there to a soul while God hides himself . . . ?"[3] It is that possibility of the loss of the sense of the "face of God" that we now address.

The gospel of the sovereign grace of God reveals that certain of fallen humanity have nevertheless been made the beneficiaries of the redemption and rescue that God set forth in his Son. But what is to be said of the progress in life of those who are redeemed by that substitutionary life and death of Christ? The question is asked because the confessions we have cited state clearly the twofold implication for the condition of the new-born person in Christ. First, in the same way as we have seen the ground on which, in the case of the natural offspring of Adam, God has withdrawn "the light of his countenance" from the sinner, so, it must now be impressed on the Christian believer, *God may, and as occasion warrants he does, withdraw the light of his countenance from his own new-born and redeemed child.* We need to discover why that may be so, and what are its possible causes, effects, and remedies. Second, the grounds of that warrant are spelled out in the fact that Christian believers, "those that are justified, and although they can never fall from the state of justification . . ." may nevertheless "by their sins fall under God's fatherly displeasure."[4] A twofold reality defines the Christian condition and possibility. First, the redeemed person who is in fact now safe in Christ may sin; and second, God may as a result withdraw from that person the light of his countenance.

THE CHRISTIAN'S STATUS AND PROGRESS

To establish the context in which the fact and the consequences of sin in the life of the Christian believer are to be addressed we summarize three aspects of what is involved. *First*, the Christian may commit precisely the same sin that was the sin of our first parents. The Christian may, that is to say, commit the sin of the assumption of autonomy, the assumption of autonomy as to being, knowledge, and behavior. Startling as that may seem, the respects in which that can and does occur in the Christian life call for careful reflection. *Second*, the effects and implications of that for the on-going Christian life and experience are manifold and need to be

3. Owen, "Of the Mortification of Sin in Believers," in *Works*, vol. 6, 53.
4. Westminster Confession, XI, 5.

recognized. And *third*, it follows that the reasons why such a condition of God's withdrawing the consciousness of his presence may occur, and the remedial action that is called for on the part of the Christian, need investigation. We shall address in turn each of those aspects of the Christian's situation and possible condition.

THE SIN OF ASSUMED AUTONOMY

The question of sin in the life of the believer is most effectively considered against the facts and meaning of the believer's true identity. What, then, is to be understood as essential to his status, and what does that hold in prospect for his on-going life in the faith to which he is now committed? First, as to his status, the biblical data repeatedly put the answer in such propositional statements as the following: "Know ye not that . . . ye are not your own? . . . ye are bought with a price" (1 Cor. 6:19–20); and "I live; yet not I, but Christ liveth in me; and the life which I now live in the flesh I live by the faith of the Son of God, who loved me, and gave himself for me" (Gal. 2:20). And second, as to the Christian's conduct and achievement in life, our Lord stated in the supper discourse on the night on which he was betrayed, "without me ye can do nothing" (John 15:5). That sets the Christian status in the shortest terms. The Christian believer is now joined to Christ, and the reality of his life is such that without Christ, apart from the presence of Christ, he can do nothing. The Christian knows that he is "not sufficient . . . to think anything as of [himself]; but [his] sufficiency is of God" (2 Cor. 3:5). The Christian believer, by virtue of the regenerating grace of God, is a new person in Christ Jesus and it can only be said of him that "he is a new creature; old things are passed away . . . all things are become new" (2 Cor. 5:17). In his sovereign and unsolicited act of regeneration God by his Spirit has conveyed to the sinner a definitive transference from the realm of sin, condemnation, and death to the realm of righteousness, justification, and life.[5] The person who is the beneficiary of that sovereign act of grace has been "delivered from the power of darkness and . . . translated into the kingdom of [God's] dear Son" (Col. 1:13).

In short, the Christian believer is now joined to Christ in a vital, spiritual, and indissoluble union. And it is consequently impossible to define or conceive of the Christian status except in terms of that union. We have already commented on the existential status of Adam, our first parent, as

---

5. See the discussion in Murray, *Romans*, vol. 1, 179.

he came from the hands of his Creator. As the image of God, he stood in a covenantal relation with God, and that relation carried with it obligations and mandates which, by his fall into sin, he repudiated. But Adam was not joined to Christ in the manner and respect in which that mysterious status is now accorded the Christian believer. That is the thrust of the apostle's claim to the Romans when he argued that "where sin abounded, grace did much more abound" (Rom. 5:20). The regenerating grace of God does not simply and only reverse the effects of sin and Adam's fall as that led to the human condition of estrangement from God and from all eternal good. By regenerating grace the Christian believer is not simply raised to the state that Adam enjoyed before he fell. He is raised to a much higher estate. Grace more abounded. And the respect in which grace more abounded is that the believer is now indissolubly joined to Christ. Adam would have been raised to the state of indefectible union with God had he not fallen and repudiated his covenantal obligations. He was the possessor of God's covenanted promise to that effect. But now that such a possibility was lost by Adam's dereliction, and now that for God's elect all of the conditions necessarily precedent to it have been fulfilled by Christ as the sinner's substitute, the Christian is the beneficiary of what Adam might have enjoyed. He no longer stands in a distanced relation to God in which a gulf of unreconcilable identity exists between them. God by his Spirit has come to the believer, and nothing can now be said about such a person except against the fact that he is existentially joined to God in Christ.

What we are about to address is to be considered against that reality of the believer's union with Christ. First, as we have just seen, the believer's union with Christ has raised him to an estate far higher than that which Adam enjoyed. Adam was defectible in a sense in which the Christian now is not. But second, there remains within the Christian a factor of inherent disturbance, a principle of indwelling sin, that did not characterize Adam in his pristine state. Third, the question has been raised in the history of doctrine whether the union with Christ that is now envisaged is to be understood as a "union of representation" or a "union of identity."[6] In reality, it is more than the former and less than the latter. It is true that the believer's union with Christ does not amount to or imply the divinization of man. And it is equally true that Christ is our representative, against our prior representation by Adam. But more than representation is involved.

---

6. See Buchanan, *Justification*, 159.

For the believer, in his new life in union with Christ is the beneficiary of the residence within him of the Holy Spirit whom Christ has sent. The apostle has made that clear, "Christ liveth in me" (Gal. 2:20).

That mysterious reality, which will be explored more fully in the following chapter, brings its import to bear on the question with which we began. That is the question of whether, and if so when and why, the "light of the countenance of God" may be turned from the person who, as has been said, lives in the context of that indissoluble union with God in Christ. We now reflect, therefore, on the respects in which the benefits and blessings of that union *may be tarnished by the same sin* that occasioned our first parent's fall, namely his assumption of autonomy.

Counter-intuitive though it may seem, and shattering though its implications might be, the foolishness of sin in the life of the believer amounts in essence to the very same defection. The believer may all too easily and sadly assert his autonomy from the God who has saved him. He may assert his autonomy, as we have seen, on the levels of being, knowledge, and behavior.

Adam, we have said, asserted his metaphysical autonomy from God. What that meant was that he asserted that he was not dependent on God for the fact and the meaning of his life. It can be said more expansively that his fall was not a metaphysical lapse, in that it did not effect any change in his metaphysical status. He remained, after his fall, a person in the image of God, a rational, immortal, spiritual, and moral person who continued to sustain covenantal obligations to God, even though he was, in his new condition, disabled from discharging those obligations. Adam's fall was, rather, an ethical lapse, in that on the level of behavior he did something he ought not to have done. He ate the forbidden fruit. His fall did not cause any change in his essential state of being. But it did have the damning implications with which we are familiar for his on-going life as estranged from God and for the eternal prospects he confronted as a result.

Now the gospel of grace explains that Christian regeneration effects a reversal of that fallen condition. While that is so, however, more than a mere reversal is involved. Against the Adamic condition, two things are to be said. First, regeneration, as we saw in a previous context, does not effect any change in one's metaphysical status or state of being. The new-born person who is joined to Christ is the image of God, a rational, immortal, spiritual, and moral person, who is still responsibly accountable to God for his life and conduct, but who has become the beneficiary of a change in his capacities of soul in terms of which that accountability and responsibility are discharged. By reason of those new endowments of soul, the Christian believer is now capable of pleasing God, of living righteously in relation to the law of God that is his rule of life, and of holding an assured prospect of eternal inheritance in the presence of God in Christ. That newly established status, we have said, exists, and the outworking of its effects in the Christian's life is possible, because such an individual is now joined to Christ. That mysterious union is what it is because Christ has sent his Spirit, the Holy Spirit whom it is possible the Christian's sin can grieve (Eph. 4:30), into residence in the soul of the believer. As the eighteenth-century evangelical, Henry Scougal, put it, the grace of regeneration establishes "the life of God in the soul of man."[7]

Second, we bring together now what we have observed as the essential Adamic sin and the essence of sin in the life of the believer that turns the "light of the countenance of God" from the Christian in his walk and life. Adam asserted that he was independent of God. That, precisely and sadly, is what the believer is all too easily capable of doing. That is what lies at the root of all Christian unhappiness and disjointedness and ineffectiveness in life. The Christian too easily forgets his elevated status as we have already connoted it *and he imagines that he can proceed in belief and conduct independently of God to whom he is, in actual fact, indissolubly joined.* That is the paradox of the Christian life. The Christian can too easily forget who he is now that God has effected his saving change within him. But the urgent question that confronts us is how that remarkable lapse from true existential reality can be brought about.

At a minimum, the Christian can fall carelessly prey to the imagination that he can proceed with his life in this world without a conscious and consistent submission to the law of God and to the direction of Christ and his Word. He forgets his Lord's reminder that "without me ye can do nothing." The Christian is too readily capable of imagining that he can live as a branch severed from the vine (John 15:1–7). But why, and how, should that be so? How can the Christian so easily forget the status to which he has been raised and the benefits that are therefore to be jealously guarded?

The reason for what we have remarked as the sin of assumed autonomy, of proceeding independently of God, is twofold and is well known to the one who is practiced in the Word of God and in the Christian life.

---

7. Scougal, *The Life of God in the Soul of Man.*

First, the allurements of sin external to the Christian exert their pressure to capitulate to old habits and desires; and second, there remains in the believer a disposition or principle of action which has been explained as the principle of indwelling sin. The apostle was eloquent on the point in the seventh chapter of his letter to the Romans. We have said that the grace of regeneration endows the faculties of the soul with abilities they did not previously possess. The believer is thereby enabled to live by godly action. We must see also that regeneration endows the soul with a new principle of action or, as we saw Robert Dabney put it, a new *habitus*. But we have seen also that a sinful principle or capacity to sin remains. In the preceding chapter we saw that John Owen had characterized the *habitus* as a "contrary habitual principle."

FURTHER EFFECTS AND IMPLICATIONS OF THE SIN OF ASSUMED AUTONOMY

The foregoing has put in place virtually all that is necessary in order to understand that sin in the regenerate person, the sin that causes God to withdraw the light of his countenance, is the same in essence as the sin of our first parent that "brought death into the world, and all our woe."[8] It remains to recall briefly that Adam's sin involved further the assertion of epistemological and ethical autonomy. By that we mean, first, the assumption that one is not dependent for criteria of truth in knowledge and understanding on what God has revealed; and secondly, that one is similarly free to establish his own criteria of action and behavior. It is a short but comprehending statement to say that all sin is the transgression of the law of God (1 John 3:4). The moral law, or the law in its moral aspect as it was given to Moses, remains the rule of life for the Christian believer. But action in fact, willing behavior, or the expression of the volitional faculty of the soul, is not in any sense the undetermined act of the will. It is always and necessarily the act of the whole person as that is motivated by the deliberations of the mind and the affections of the heart as communicated to the will.[9] Jonathan Edwards argued cogently in his eighteenth-century work on the freedom of the will that "every act of the will is some

8. Milton, *Paradise Lost*, line 3.

9. For a more extensive discussion of the will see Vickers, *Divine Redemption*, 74–105.

way connected with the understanding."[10] He understood that the will cannot determine its own action (as the Arminianism that Edwards set out to controvert had claimed) but that its action is determined by the interdependent motivations of all of the faculties of the soul. In the case of the unregenerate, for example, the act of the will is dependent on what Edwards referred to as the "bias" of the soul, the "certain deformity in the nature of the dispositions and acts of the heart,"[11] "the total depravity and corruption of man's nature, whereby his heart is wholly under the power of sin."[12] We now see that it is precisely the remnants of that same proclivity or principle of action, or the disposition or *habitus* as Dabney referred to it, that lies at the root also of sin in the Christian believer.

When we refer now to the *sin of assumed epistemic autonomy* in the believer we are not speaking of any defectiveness in the laws of logic that determine the result of regenerate reasoning. The laws of logic are the same for the believer and the unbeliever.[13] They are God-endowed forms of logical sequence and validity. What we have in view is the fact that the unbeliever will automatically make use of those laws of reasoning against apostate presuppositions that deny the sovereignty of God in the specification of criteria of truth. At this point we observe again the pressure of the bias in the soul, here coming to expression in false presuppositions and thereby invalidating the search for truth before the journey into understanding even gets under way.

The Christian believer, it is now being said, is capable of falling into the same sin of imagining that he can discover true meaning on whatever level of discourse might engage him without consciously referring to the principles of interpretation that God has laid down. The issue becomes that of the efficient criteria of truth and true meaning. The Christian is sadly capable of forgetting that "in [Christ] are hid all the treasures of wisdom and knowledge" (Col. 2:3). It would be a larger task than can detain us at this point to explore the fuller meaning of what has just been said. But the principle remains, and its significance remains determinative, that an all too frequent source of sin in the believer is the failure to refer all things, on all levels of understanding and in all areas of belief and behav-

10. Edwards, *Freedom of the Will*, 86.

11. Ibid., 341.

12. Ibid., 325.

13. See Van Til, *Common Grace*, 27–28. See also the same author's *Christian Theory of Knowledge*, passim.

ior, to the criteria that God has provided in his word. That fact in itself leads to the relevance to the Christian life of the third level of assumed autonomy, that of ethical criteria.

Essentially, the Christian can too easily fall into sin on the grounds we have now adduced. He can forget that his life is what it is, and his belief and actions should be what they are because, as we have explored already, he is joined to Christ in an indissoluble union. Sin in the Christian exists in his forgetting to allow belief and action to be determined by the implications of that existential reality. If, as is the case, one is joined to Christ, then his belief and actions should be determined by what the apostle explained to the Galatians in his claim that "I live, yet not I, but Christ liveth in me" (Gal. 2:20). In that, we are not speaking of any mystical or monastic resignation to an irrational or non-rational spiritual motive that distances the life of the mind from that of the emotions and the heart. At the same time as we confirm, where that is necessary, the value of a true Christian mysticism (for all the doctrines of our faith terminate in mystery) we are saying at this point that the Christian faith calls for a reasoned understanding that is firmly grounded for the regenerate mind in the revelation of truth that God has made. That revelation inheres in the Word he has spoken and preserved for us in the Scriptures, and paramountly in his Son who came into the world to be our redeemer. Christian action, then, is to be determined by the criteria that God's law has adequately provided.

The Christian is required consciously to avoid the temptation to assumed autonomy on the level of belief (the specification of his own criteria of truth) and on the level of behavior (the self-formulated specification of criteria of action). He bows to the truth and veracity of our Lord's promise that "when he, the Spirit of truth, is come, he will guide you into all truth" (John 16:13). Christ in his Word has articulated clearly all the necessary criteria of truth, on the levels of being, knowledge, and behavior, and the Christian believer will energetically pursue his grasp and understanding of all aspects of the truth, and the criteria of truth, that God has given.

It is unnecessary to advert at length in our present context to the extensive Scriptural arguments as to the legitimate place of reason in the Christian life. We have been more directly concerned with the danger of a misplaced reliance on the competence of reason, particularly in its unregenerate and ungodly form and expression, and with the danger of the Christian believer's relapse and misplaced capitulation to its aims and claims. The Scriptures are replete with statements of the relevant warnings and dangers. "Beware lest any man spoil you [take you captive] through philosophy and vain deceit, after the tradition of men, after the rudiments of the world, and not after Christ" (Col. 2:8). And the same apostle had written extensively to the Corinthian church regarding the "wisdom of this world" that God made "foolish" by the foolishness of the preaching of the gospel of grace (1 Cor. 1:19–21). To the contrary, the Christian's directive is forthright and clear and totalitarian: "Casting down imaginations, and every high thing that exalteth itself against the knowledge of God, and bringing into captivity every thought to the obedience of Christ" (2 Cor. 10:5).

The Christian is warned against the danger of misplaced epistemic criteria and is required to understand, not the necessity of avoiding the action of the mind and relapsing into some kind of emotional or mystical absorption or preoccupation, but the legitimacy and necessity of reasoning with and by the regenerate mind. For the grace of regeneration is effective in the renewing of the mind. Old forms of enquiry and presuppositions are done away. "Be not conformed to this world," the apostle has said, "but be ye transformed by the renewing of your mind, that ye may prove what is that good, and acceptable, and perfect will of God" (Rom. 12:2). Indeed, it is of the essence of the Scriptural call for repentance and faith that the first appeal of the gospel is to the mind. For the essence of the call to repentance is the command to think again, to rethink, now under the impulse and enlightenment of the Holy Spirit, the meaning of one's condition, his lostness in sin apart from God, and the mercy of the Savior whom he now sees set forth by God for his relief.

Further, it would be productive, as throwing light on the true place of reason in the Christian life and awareness, to advert to the expressive argument of the great Dutch theologian, Abraham Kuyper. In very brief terms, Kuyper argued, in the context of his study of the meaning and effects of God's common grace, not for an abdication of all forms of reason, but for the understanding of what he referred to as "two kinds of people" and the diverging significances of those two classes. He had in view the regenerate on the one hand and the unregenerate on the other. That is, of course, the basic dichotomization that informs true Christian understanding and categories of explanation. Following his discussion on that basic level, Kuyper spoke extensively of the meaning and implications of regeneration, or what he referred to as *palingenesis*, and argued further that as there were two kinds of people, so there were two kinds of science. There is science that understands it is investigating God-established facts that are extant and cohere in accordance with God-created laws of function and operation; and there is science that imagines it is investigating random, brute, and chance-determined facts that are explicable in terms of autonomous impersonal laws.[14]

Van Til has argued in similar fashion: "It is either the would-be autonomous man, who weighs and measures what he thinks of as brute or bare facts by the help of what he thinks of as abstract impersonal principles, or it is the believer, knowing himself to be a creature of God, who weighs and measures what he thinks of as God-created facts by what he thinks of as God-created laws."[15] Kuyper and Van Til have directed us to the meaning of bringing every thought captive to Christ.

TEMPTATION AND RELIEF

A critical issue remains to be addressed, one that strikes to the heart of the doctrinal agenda we have proposed. We are interested at this point in the fact of temptation to sin, temptation, for example, to the dangerous sins of assumed autonomy that have engaged us to this point. If, as we have said, the Christian believer is in fact joined to Christ in a union that makes his title to heaven secure, what, if anything, is to be said of the possibility of his falling into sin beyond the limit of recovery? Two things are relevant. First, we have it on the authority of our Lord himself that of those who come to him in the faith and repentance the Spirit imparts, none of them will be lost (John 17:12). No man, no entity in all of creation, is able to pluck them out of his hand (John 10:28). And the apostle Paul has summed up the matter in his lyrical response to the question, "Who shall separate us from the love of Christ?" (Rom. 8:35). "Neither death, nor life, nor angels, nor principalities, nor powers . . . nor any other creature . . ." he responds; and the practiced Christian is familiar with the truth of the apostle's continuing claim at that point (Rom. 8:38–39). It cannot be gainsaid that the true believer is "kept by the power of God through faith unto salvation ready to be revealed in the last time" (1 Pet. 1:5). And "the Lord knoweth how to deliver the godly out of temptation" (2 Pet. 2:9).

But second, temptation does come, it will come in the believer's life, and in his present state of imperfect sanctification he will inevitably fall. We in no way, therefore, minimize the fact or the seriousness of sin. We

14. Kuyper, *Principles of Sacred Theology*, chap. 3.
15. Van Til, *Common Grace*, 44.

emphasize the meaning of sin. We are convicted of the exceeding sinfulness of sin, of what one of our Puritan fathers referred to as "The Plague of
Plagues."[16] What, then, is to be said? We have already argued that the possibility of the sin of assumed autonomy from God is to be contemplated
in the same context as one acknowledges the reality of an indissoluble
union with Christ. The sin in view is a sin in direct contradiction of the
essence of what and who the Christian believer is. It is, as it was in the case
of our first parent, a contradiction of one's essential status.

We may bring together both sides of the issue we have now raised by
reference to the argument of the apostle that "God is faithful, who will not
suffer you to be tempted above that ye are able; but will with the temptation also make a way of escape, that ye may be able to bear it" (1 Cor.
10:13). That textual statement has been the subject of varying interpretations in the history of commentary. That may follow from the fact that on
superficial appearance the verse seems not to be clearly connected to the
textual argument that either precedes or follows it. But on closer inspection it expands on the statement in context that we in our day are warned
against, and should not fall into, the sins and failings of the Israelites
which are set forth there as our examples. It is possible to say, as has been
claimed, that the foolishness of the Christian may be such that while, as
the text says, God makes available a "way of escape," the Christian simply
ignores and does not take advantage of the way that is thus provided. But
that, seemingly, is too easy an explanation and leaves too much unsaid.

Let us put the matter in the following terms. If the only thing to be
said is in agreement with the interpretation of the Corinthian text we
have referred to (1 Cor. 10:13), that the problem of the Christian is that he
ignores and does not take advantage of the escape from temptation that
God provides, we would be guilty of a complete failure to understand the
true status of the believer who has been brought to faith in Christ. For we
have claimed that it is not possible to describe or define the Christian person except by defining him as joined to Christ. But if, as is demonstrably
the case, that vital and spiritual union exists, then we must say that every
action of such a person is an action by a person who is joined to Christ. If
that person rejoices, it is the rejoicing of a person who is joined to Christ.
If that person sins, it is the sinning of a person who is joined to Christ. No
longer does there exist between God and the individual what we previ-

---

16. Venning, *The Plague of Plagues*.

ously referred to as a distanced relation of unreconcilable identity. The true believer is not now left to himself as a distanced antagonist of God. We can say nothing less than that the Sprit of God is within him and, with the apostle Paul, "Christ liveth in me" (Gal. 2:20). But the person who now stands in that high estate sins. Of course he sins. The remarkable fact is that when that person sins it is a person who is joined to Christ that sins. That is the existential fact from which there can be no escape.

The doctrinal relevance of that can be put in the following terms. Every thought and action of the true Christian believer is the thought and action of a person who is joined to Christ. The Christian person does not, and cannot, live independently of Christ to whom he is now joined. If that were not so, there would be no point in the apostle's admonition, "Grieve not the Holy Spirit of God, by whom ye are sealed unto the day of redemption" (Eph. 4:30). Again if that is so, what is to be said of the question that has principally engaged us to this point, namely the temptation to assumed autonomy from God? The true believer is capable of acting in such a way as to imply that on the levels of being, knowledge, and behavior he is effectively assuming an autonomy from God. But we now have it on the authority of God's own word and promise, as we have it also from the implication of the believer's status, that *he cannot continue to be successful in that assumption.* Because he is who he is, God by his Spirit will frustrate his very attempt to continue in sin. As the apostle John put it, "Whosoever is born of God doth not commit sin; for his seed remaineth in him; and he cannot sin [that is, he cannot consent to continue in sin], because he is born of God" (1 John 3:9). It is a remarkable fact of God's ministry to his saints that he frustrates their desires to leave him and to fall continually into sin. As John Owen puts it, "he . . . stops the course of sin."

Observe how Owen makes the point. "When lust hath conceived, and is ready to bring forth—when the soul lies at the brink of some iniquity—he [God] gives in seasonable help, relief, deliverance, and safety. Here lies a great part of the care and faithfulness of Christ towards his poor saints. He will not suffer them to be worried with the power of sin, nor to be carried out unto ways that shall dishonour the gospel, or fill them with shame and reproach, and so render them useless in the world; but he steps in with the saving relief and assistance of his grace, *stops the course of sin*, and makes them in himself more than conquerors. And this assistance lies under the promise, 1 Cor. 10:13."[17]

But when all that is said, the truth remains that in the Christian believer's flirtation with sin, and because of his carelessness in not adhering in belief and behavior to the truth and the fact that has made him who he is, God does withdraw the light of his countenance. That causes the believer's loss of joy, comfort, usefulness, and effectiveness in his service for the Lord who has saved him. It will be useful to observe a textual statement that bears on the point.

We have spoken adequately of the possibility that the true Christian believer who is indissolubly joined to Christ may temporarily fall into the sin of assumed autonomy. Consider, for example, the possibility of assumed autonomy as to knowledge and its ethical implications. We may refer to the statement of the apostle to the Ephesians that he prayed "that the God of our Lord Jesus Christ . . . may give you the spirit of wisdom and revelation in the knowledge of him . . ." (Eph. 1:17). We confront at that point the mystery of the divine Spirit's ministry to the soul of the Christian. Admittedly, differences of view have been held in the history of commentary as to whether the "spirit" in Paul's sentence refers to the human spirit (as, possibly, KJV, NKJV, and apparently ESV) or the Holy Spirit (as NIV). But our own conclusion is that the Holy Spirit is clearly intended. Suffice it to say that the same understanding is reported in, for example, Hendriksen's commentary,[18] (where reasons for the conclusion are explored at length), and is held by Lloyd-Jones who speaks of "the Spirit of wisdom" and "the Spirit of revelation"[19] by Matthew Poole,[20] and Matthew Henry,[21] and, as a matter of historic interest, by S. D. F. Salmond in *The Expositor's Greek Testament*, where it is observed in reference to the text that "It is necessary . . . to take πνεῦμα [pneuma] as = the *Holy*

17. Owen, "The Nature and Power of Indwelling Sin," in *Works*, vol. 6, 277, italics added. This statement of Owen is to be set against his comment on the same text, 1 Cor. 10:13, in his in his essay, "Of Temptation": "Though there be a sufficiency of grace provided for all the *elect*, that they shall by no temptation fall utterly from God, yet it would make any gracious heart to tremble, to think what dishonour to God, what scandal to the gospel, what woful darkness and disquietness they may bring upon their own souls, though they perish not." Op. cit., in *Works*, vol. 6, 116–17.

18. Hendriksen, *Ephesians*, 96–97.

19. Lloyd-Jones, *God's Ultimate Purpose*, 356, 360.

20. Poole, *Commentary on the Holy Bible*, vol. 3, 665.

21. Matthew Henry, Commentary ad loc. cit.

Spirit.[22] But it is not necessary to count commentators. In a simple, or-dinary, and devotional reading of the text, the reader does well to pause and consider the mystery of the Holy Spirit's working in the believer's life in such a way as to promote the growth of wisdom and knowledge. Then the question as we have addressed it in this chapter is bluntly before the Christian's mind, and his right response is calculated to provoke his worship and praise. Will the Christian, consistent with the true status of his union with Christ, maintain his dependence on the mysterious guid-ance and working of the Holy Spirit in the development of a holy wisdom through the means of grace? Or will he, on the contrary, allow a slippage at that crucial point by placing reliance on, as we have connoted it, an assumed competence of independent human reason? How, then, it must follow, will the wisdom the Holy Spirit imparts and develops be reflected on relevant ethical levels in the Christian's life and walk?

THE LOSS OF THE FACE OF GOD,
ITS CAUSES AND REMEDIES

The poverty of soul that is consequent on God's "hiding himself," to recall the expressive phrase of Owen, is well known to the serious believer. Such a condition, he has learned, follows from the sin of belief and behavior that is a reversion to the implications of a previous status and character. It im-plies subjectively a loss of joy, and objectively a loss of effectiveness and usefulness in service for the Lord who saved him and to whom, in his better moments, the believer knows he is inseparably joined. The poet of the eigh-teenth-century evangelical awakening, William Cowper, has given eloquent expression to what is involved when the believer loses, in whatever way we have now suggested is possible, the light of the face of God:

> O for a closer walk with God,
> A calm and heavenly frame;
> A light that shines upon the road
> That leads me to the lamb.
>
> Where is the blessedness I knew
> When first I saw the Lord?
> Where is the soul-refreshing view
> Of Jesus, and his word?

22. Nicoll, *Expositor's Greek Testament*, vol. 3, 273–74.

Cowper's plea was raised against the reality of the unrest of soul that is, for the time, bereft of the comfort of the realized presence of God:

> Return, O holy dove, return,
> Sweet messenger of rest;
> I hate the sins that made thee mourn
> And drove thee from my breast.[23]

But why should the "loss of the face of God" be at all possible for the truly born-again child of God? We have spoken at adequate length for our present purposes of the possibility of sin in the life of the believer, and we have summarized the nature and causes of sin under heads that bring it into relation with the first sin that cast us all down to the state of loss and potential perdition. It is not necessary to summarize again the points of that argument. But two final aspects of the causes of the loss of the light of the countenance of God should be noted. First, subjectively, it is clear that the condition of which we have spoken is traceable primarily and paramountly to a weakening of prayer in the Christian life. Adequate guidance is available in the Word of God as to the necessity and urgency, the proper forms, and the sanctifying effectiveness of the believer's consistent life of prayer. How little we know of what is required of us in prayer in order that God will be glorified and that we ourselves will grow in both our consciousness of the faith and our conformity to his image in Christ to which we are called. And how little we know experimentally of the sanctifying contributions of prayer as we purport to progress through this short, uncertain life and earthly pilgrimage to the glory that God has prepared for those who love him. Should not our prayer be for forgiveness for our laxity and lack of diligence at this very initial and basic point?

Secondly, that subjective issue aside, we must say objectively that the cause of God's hiding his face from us is that we are too readily delinquent in pursuing the means of grace he has provided for us. Those means of grace include the diligent study of the Word of God and the faithful attendance on the preaching of it, the partaking of the sacraments that have been provided for our encouragement and direction, the benefits of membership of the community of saints into which we have been called in the church, the true and proper worship, both private and corporate, and the wider benefits of admission to the unique culture of the church,

---

23. Cowper, *O for a closer walk with God*, Congregational Praise, 476.

which, properly understood, is in its varied aspects antithetical to the culture of the world.

CONCLUSION

Before making a concluding statement, several propositions summarize much of what has been said.

First, the essence of our first parent's sin was his assertion of autonomy against God. That was the sin by which Satan had fallen. In Adam's case it involved the repudiation of his covenantal obligations.

Second, that false assertion of autonomy was expressed on the levels of being, knowledge, and behavior (ontology, epistemology, and ethics). In place of God-established laws of being and function it assumed that criteria of validity and truth in knowing, and of rules of right and wrong behavior, could be efficiently established by the individual.

Third, the Christian believer is capable of committing, and he does commit, the very same sin of assumed autonomy, again on the levels of being, knowledge, and behavior.

Fourth, in doing so, the Christian denies his true identity. The Christian's sin is a contradiction of his essential status.

Fifth, as God withdrew the light of his countenance from sinful Adam, so he can, and he does as occasion warrants, withdraw the light of his countenance from the Christian believer. That means, not the withdrawal of his Spirit, by whom the Christian is joined to Christ in an indissoluble union, but the withdrawal of the awareness, the consciousness, and the heart-warming sensibility of his presence.

Sixth, the Christian believer is joined to God in Christ in a respect in which prelapsarian Adam was not. The Christian has been introduced to a status higher than Adam enjoyed, but to which Adam would have attained had he sustained his probation.

Seventh, the Christian can, and though it is counter-intuitive he does, forget his elevated status and imagine that he can proceed in belief and conduct independently of God to whom he is, in fact, indissolubly joined.

Eighth, the Christian's sin of assumed autonomy is the sin of a person who is joined to Christ. All he does and thinks is done and thought by a person who is joined to Christ. If he rejoices, it is the rejoicing of a person joined to Christ. If he sins, it is the sin of a person joined to Christ.

Ninth, it is impossible for the true Christian believer to break the bond of union with Christ in which the Holy Spirit of God has established him.

Tenth, God, in the light of that impossibility and in faithfulness to his sworn covenant, will, as John Owen has put it, stop the course of sin.

The paragraph of the Westminster Confession we cited at the beginning goes on to state that those from whom the "light of his countenance" has been withdrawn for any of the reasons and causes we have contemplated will "not have the light of his countenance restored unto them, until they humble themselves, confess their sins, beg pardon, and renew their faith and repentance."[24] Consider the anguish of the spouse in the Song of Solomon, "I sought him whom my soul loveth; I sought him, but I found him not" (Song 3:1). The beloved had withdrawn. Should we not show the same diligence in wanting his company, in seeking him, and rejoicing again in the discovery of him and the comfort of his grace? We have it on the authority of the Word of God that "If we confess our sins, he is faithful and just to forgive us our sins, and to cleanse us from all unrighteousness" (1 John 1:9).

But we know that the ground of that forgiveness is not our repentance. The only ground on which our joy and comfort in Christ exists is the completed redemptive work, the active and passive obedience, that he provided on our behalf in this world. Let us, forsaking all else, go out to him and find him ever again. Let us be anxious to be like him and to honor him in the service of affection that we poor and needy sinners can give to him.

We have considered the possible causes, effects, and remedies of the sorry condition of losing the sight of "the face of God." We know that in the last great day, when "there shall be no more curse . . . [we] shall see his face" (Rev. 22:3–4). But the glory of the gospel is that now, though we walk, perchance, in a vale of shadows and tears, we have the "earnest," the down payment, of our inheritance (Eph. 1:14). May we therefore give all diligence to know him as he waits to reveal himself to us ever more closely. God grant that it may be so.

---

24. Westminster Confession, XI, 5.

7

Adoption and Union with Christ

IN THE HISTORY OF theological controversy, doctrinal innovations have frequently troubled the church, disturbing its peace and challenging its purity. But it is beyond doubt that in the providence of God the clarification and codification of the church's belief have been the beneficial offsprings of debates within its councils. The response to the Arian and Sabellian controversies in the early centuries, the magnificent defense of the Nicean orthodoxy by Athanasius, the culmination of the Christological settlement at Chalcedon in 451, Augustine's defeat of Pelagian claims, and the Reformation's rebuttal of the semi-Pelagianism of Rome—from all such doctrinal disturbances has come a sharpening of theological perception and sensitivity. As a result, the biblical revelation has been understood more clearly and the deposit of truth preserved.

But new disturbances haunt the theological landscape. At this time of day, and in the context of swirling debates that have absorbed academic and ecclesiastical energies, it is unnecessary to observe at length that the biblical-Reformed doctrine of justification has come under heavy attack. That the sinner whom the Spirit of God brings to repentance and faith is justified, or is accounted righteous, by a declarative-forensic-judicial statement of God, has become subject to widely varying interpretations. Not all claims in the contemporary literature can be sustained as "good and necessary consequences" of the biblical data.[1] The doctrinal claims of the so-called New Perspective on Paul, Shepherdism, and the Federal Vision Theology have been widely critiqued and do not call for extended

---

1. See Westminster Confession, I, 6: "The whole counsel of God, concerning all things necessary for his own glory, man's salvation, faith, and life, is either expressly set down in scripture, or by *good and necessary consequences* may be deduced from scripture." Italics added.

rehearsal at this time.[2] We shall return to some aspects of them later in this chapter. It remains true that as Luther referred to the doctrine of justification, it must still be seen as "the article of faith that decides whether the church is standing or falling."[3] But it is necessary to recognize that as a result of disturbances on these levels, certain ancillary and cognate doctrines have been either diminished in importance or presented in ways that misrepresent their place in the theological corpus. Certain forms of contemporary debate suggest that the doctrines of adoption and the believer's union with Christ are in danger of such a diminution and misrepresentation.

In the following sections we shall expand the reference in the preceding chapter to the Christian believer's union with Christ. After an initial statement of the doctrine and an indication of some relevant doctrinal loci, note will be taken of some problematic implications of recent theological emphases. At that stage it will be possible to draw attention to some aspects of the significance for the on-going Christian life of the related doctrines of adoption and union with Christ.

THE DOCTRINE OF UNION WITH CHRIST

Union with Christ is a principal benefit and bequest to the soul by virtue of the salvation wrought by Christ in the perfect redemptive work he accomplished. That work was in fulfillment of the divine purpose of salvation, and it realized the objectives of the covenant of redemption that had been established in the council of the Godhead before the foundation of the world. To make that statement is to acknowledge the comprehensive and, in many respects, the all-determining significance of union with Christ in the divine purpose of salvation. Union with Christ, as John Murray has observed, is "a very broad and embracive subject. . . . [I]n its broader aspects it underlies every step of the application of redemption. Union with Christ is really the central truth of the whole doctrine of salvation not only in its application but also in its once-for-all accomplishment in the finished work of Christ."[4] The force of that truth follows from the

---

2. See references in chapter 1 at footnote 5. Valuable critiques of the doctrinal positions referred to are contained in Reports issued by Committees of the Presbyterian Church in America and the Orthodox Presbyterian Church. See the bibliography below.

3. See Buchanan, *Justification*, vii.

4. Murray, *Redemption*, 201.

fact that the subjects of the redemptive covenant were chosen "in Christ" (Eph. 1:4–5). The very fountain of salvation resides in union with Christ. For that reason the apostle goes on to say to the Ephesians that it is "in the beloved" that "we have redemption through his blood" (Eph. 1:6–7).

But it will be observed more fully in a moment that the believer's union with Christ is closely and vitally associated with the Holy Spirit's conveyance to God's elect of the grace of regeneration. The Westminster Shorter Catechism, in answer to the question, "How are we made partakers of the redemption purchased by Christ?" states that it is accomplished "by the effectual application of it to us by his Holy Spirit."[5] The question arises, then, as to how the Holy Spirit does, in fact, apply the benefits of Christ's redemption. It comes to effect, the Catechism states, by the Spirit's "working faith in us, and thereby *uniting us to Christ* in our effectual calling"[6] The *uniting to Christ* is there conceived of as an aspect of what is involved in God's effectual calling of the sinner to salvation. The matter has been taken further in expressive terms by the Savoy Declaration of Faith, the Congregational confession of 1658 that followed and substantially adhered to the Westminster Confession of Faith of 1647. Both of those important documents include chapter 13, "Of Sanctification." The Savoy refers there to "[Those] that are effectually called and regenerated, *being united to Christ . . .*"[7] The italicized phrase is omitted from the Westminster Confession, and its inclusion in the Savoy is an example of the keenness of perception among the seventeenth-century Puritans as to the comprehensive import of union with Christ. Further examination will show that both the confessional documents we have referred to, in their parallel chapters on God's eternal decrees, effectual calling, adoption, and sanctification, hold a similarly high view of the determinative import of union with Christ.[8]

It is well known that what is referred to in current doctrinal terminology as regeneration was placed by the seventeenth-century authors within the wider scope of what they understood as effectual calling. The latter, it is clear, ranges from the initiatory convicting work of the Holy

5. Westminster Shorter Catechism, Question 29.

6. Ibid., question 30, italics added.

7. Savoy Declaration, XIII, 1, italics added.

8. When reference is made to the Westminster Confession of Faith and the Savoy Declaration of Faith it should be noted that similar statements are included in the Second London (Baptist) Confession of 1689.

Spirit in the soul, "convincing us of our sin and misery, enlightening our minds in the knowledge of Christ, and renewing our wills," to the sinner's "embrace [of] Jesus Christ freely offered to us in the gospel."[9] Within that wider range of saving effects we recognize what we refer to as the Holy Spirit's work of regeneration. That, it can be said by way of summary and to recall the definition we have given, is a sovereign, unsolicited act of God, a work of his free grace, whereby the faculties of the soul are endowed with abilities and capacities they did not previously possess and by which a new disposition or principle of holy action is implanted in the soul. The important Dutch Reformed theologian, Wilhelmus à Brakel, who was prominent in the Dutch Second Reformation in the seventeenth century, grasped the same conception of the effects of the grace of regeneration. He observes in relation to the beneficiaries of that grace that "Their mind, will, and affections have been changed. They have become new creatures . . . in consequence of this change wrought within the soul . . ."[10] "When the moment of good pleasure arrives for each of the elect . . . the Holy Spirit quickens and grants him spiritual life, *this being the consequence of the soul's union with God in Christ.*"[11] In that statement two quite distinct things are being said. First, it is stated that there is the close association between regeneration and union with Christ that we have referred to. But second, it is clarified in the italicized phrase that union with Christ is not to be understood properly as the *result* of regeneration, but as the accompanying reality, or rather, as the more remote and embracive action of God from which, as we have already seen Murray claim, all aspects and elements of salvation flow.

John Owen, a foremost English language theologian of the same century, effectively made a similar point: "No person, therefore, whatever, who hath not been made partaker of the washing of regeneration and the renovation of the Holy Ghost, can possibly have any union with Christ."[12] Owen continues, by way of clarifying that statement: "I do not speak of this as though our purifying were in order of time and nature antecedent unto our union with Christ, for indeed it is an effect thereof."[13] There is a

---

9. Westminster Shorter Catechism, question 31.

10. à Brakel, *Christian's Reasonable Service*, vol. 1, 183.

11. Idem, italics added.

12. Owen, *Pneumatologia*, 464.

13. Idem.

sense, Owen says, which is to be clearly understood, in which regeneration is an "effect" of our union with Christ. In the purpose and provision of God, that is to say, the believer's union with Christ is the comprehensive reality that informs and determines all of the elements and aspects of the salvation of God's elect. In further comments on the "work of the Spirit of God upon us in our regeneration," Owen states that "This is that whereby we have *union with Jesus Christ*, the head of the church. Originally and *efficiently* the Holy Spirit dwelling in him and us is the cause of this union; but *formally* this new principle of grace is so."[14]

Bringing together the issues we have raised, it can be said by way of further summary that by virtue of God's sovereign act of regeneration in the soul there comes to full and pre-ordained awareness in the Christian believer the reality that he or she is now joined to Christ in an organic, vital, spiritual, and indissoluble union. When we asked the question in an earlier chapter whether the union contemplated is a "union of representation" or a "union of identity,"[15] we observed that it is more than the former and less than the latter. It is true that the believer's union with Christ does not amount to or imply the divinization of man. It is not, and cannot be, a union of identity. Union with Christ does not take up the communication to the individual of the essential properties of the Godhead or participation in the divine essence. It does not convey to the new-born sinner any aspect of the incommunicable attributes of God. It is true, as the apostle Peter has stated it, that the beneficiary of God's grace of regeneration is made a "partaker of the divine nature" (2 Pet. 1:4). But in view at that point is the fact that regeneration conveys to the individual aspects of the communicable attributes of God, and that by the on-going progress of sanctification that has begun in regeneration those graces are further developed. God, who is sovereign in all aspects of salvation, in regeneration, justification, and sanctification, conveys to his people the grace of his communicable attributes to the extent that, and in the degree that, he is preparing them for the place he has ordained they will occupy in the eternal kingdom of glory.

It is equally true that Christ is our representative, against our prior representation by Adam. In that respect the union with Christ is, it is true, one of representation. But more than representation is involved. For the

---

14. Ibid., 477–78.

15. See Buchanan, *Justification*, 159.

believer, in his new life in union with Christ, is the beneficiary of the residence within him of the Holy Spirit whom Christ has sent. The apostle has made that clear when he says, "Christ liveth in me" (Gal. 2:20). On the night on which he was betrayed Christ said to his disciples, "I will not leave you comfortless; I will come to you" (John 14:18), and that promise was fulfilled on the day of Pentecost when Christ came by his Holy Spirit to dwell in a full and continuing presence with his people.

When we say that the union contemplated is "organic," we have in view the fact that the union connotes and carries with it union within the organic body of the church that Christ has redeemed. The church is joined to him as the body is to the head, receiving from him all necessary life-sustaining power and influence. The union carries with it and implies, moreover, not only union with Christ who is the Head of the church, but union also with other beneficiaries of Christ's redemption who comprise the church. For the church was elect in Christ before the foundation of the world and is now called into union in and with him.

The union, we have said also, is a "vital and spiritual" union. That conveys the fact that it is a union that is consummated by the Holy Spirit and that communicates to the believer life, both present and continuing until the eternal day of glory dawns. The Christian believer's status and his on-going life in Christ is what it is because it is instigated at his new birth (John 3:5–8) and is sustained in his life journey by the ministry of the Spirit of Christ.

Finally, we have said that the union is "indissoluble." By that, two things are meant. First, as has just been said, the union is indissoluble in that it will be maintained by the grace of God until and throughout eternity. But more particularly, it is indissoluble because, as we shall explore more fully, it is a substantial union with Christ by his Spirit, the breaking of which would imply nothing less than the dismemberment of the relation between Christ and his people that was established definitively in the predeterminate counsel of God. To say that the union was dissoluble would be to dismember the body of Christ. Christ cannot be divided. And now that he has been joined in substantial and spiritual union with his people, the Christ-church union that exists cannot be divided. God's eternally stated purpose of the redemption of his elect, with the sworn commitment and undertaking of the Persons of the Godhead to bring to effect all that was thereby contemplated and promised, is inviolable.

We might anticipate at this point something of what is involved for the believer by virtue of the union with Christ that has thus been sovereignly established. à Brakel has observed that "This union is therefore real, essential, true, complete, without any reservation, eternally inseparable, spiritual."[16] The Scriptural data are copious. "Know ye not that ye are the temple of God, and that the Spirit of God dwelleth in you?" (1 Cor. 3:16). Of the beneficiary of the union it is said that "My Father shall love him, and we will come unto him, and make our abode with him" (John 14:23). "He that is joined to the Lord is one spirit" (1 Cor. 6:17). "[Ye have] put on the Lord Jesus Christ" (Rom. 13:14). "Rooted and built up in him [Christ]" (Col. 2:7). "That they also may be one in us . . . I in them" (John 17:21, 23). "Know ye not your own selves, how that Jesus Christ is in you" (2 Cor. 13:5). "For as many of you as have been baptized into Christ have put on Christ" (Gal. 3:27). "God . . . hath raised us up together, and made us sit together in heavenly places in Christ Jesus" (Eph. 2:4, 6).

It will reinforce the comprehensive significance of our union with Christ to observe the following. Not only, as has been said, were the elect of God chosen in Christ (Eph. 1:4), but they were united with him in all the aspects of the work of redemption that he accomplished for them. They were crucified with him (Rom. 6:6; Gal. 3:27); "buried with him in baptism, wherein also ye are risen with him" (Col. 2:12); and as Murray has observed, believers have fallen asleep in Christ and will rise in Christ (1 Thess. 4:14, 16), and with Christ they will be glorified (Rom. 8:17).[17] Further, it follows from the Scriptural data that union with Christ involves union with the three Persons of the Godhead. Staggering as the thought and realization may be, it would be a diminution beyond the bounds of responsibility to overlook the fact that the mystical union we are now addressing carries with it nothing less than union with the triune Persons of the Godhead, the Father, the Son, and the Holy Spirit. The union, as has been said, is not one of identity. The believer is not, by reason of the union, divinized. But being more than a union of representation it is a real and vital and spiritual union. Without a careful recognition of the terms of that union it is not possible to describe or define the Christian person and the eternal prospects and inheritance that he enjoys.

16. à Brakel, *Christian's Reasonable Service*, vol. 2, 89.
17. See Murray, *Redemption*, 203–204.

A CONTEMPORARY RESPONSE

The question of the believer's union with Christ has become the subject of controversy in contemporary theological discussion. It is necessary to reflect, therefore, on both the nature and benefits of the union itself and the grounds on which, in the light of all that the eternal counsel of God had purposed, those benefits are conveyed to the believer. Inherent in that divine purpose was the perfect redemptive work that Christ accomplished, and all of the benefits that accrue to the believer find their grounding in his substitutionary work. Those benefits and blessings include, as Berkhof refers to it, the "subjective realization"[18] of the union with Christ that is brought to effect in actual historic time. It is the divine view of the justificatory complex inherent in Christ's redemptive offering that makes possible the conveyance to the sinner of the graces of regeneration, union with Christ, justification, sanctification, and the believer's final glorification.

The theology that has descended from the Reformation has traced out "the doctrine of the application of the work of redemption,"[19] or the *ordo salutis*, in those terms. At the very basis of the *ordo* the establishment of union with Christ has been understood as closely associated with God's act of regeneration within the soul. In his *Systematic Theology*, Berkhof has judiciously placed his chapters on "The Mystical Union" and "Regeneration and Effectual Calling" before that on "Justification." It would therefore appear to be a misreading of Berkhof to refer, as Horton does, to his "summary of the Reformed position on mystical union as the *result* rather than the *source* of justification."[20] Horton's construction of the *ordo salutis* rests on the frequently stated claim that "we are united to Christ through faith [which is] the source . . . of justification."[21] He apparently understands by that, not that God's establishment of the union is made possible by the work of Christ that results in our justification, but that it is actually in the act of justification that the union itself, and not the subjective realization of it, is effected. Horton observes that "justification . . . is the forensic basis of union;"[22] "it

---

18. Berkhof, *Systematic Theology*, 450.

19. Ibid., 12.

20. Horton, *Covenant and Salvation*, 197, italics added.

21. Ibid., 147.

22. Ibid., 129.

is the forensic origin of our union with Christ";[23] "Forensic justification through faith alone is the fountain of union with Christ."[24] Horton argues that "Justification [is] the judicial basis for mystical union"[25] or is "the legal ground of mystical union."[26] But those statements may properly be made only if we are holding clearly in view the "forensic" or the "legal" grounds of what is involved; if, that is to say, our focus is on the divine transaction that lies behind justification, namely the divine recognition of the merit of the substitutionary work of Christ that establishes the ground of God's dealings with man in the matter of his salvation. But apart from a focus on such grounds, it is necessary to take full biblical account of the terms and the processes in which God's dealings with man actually occur. A distinction is to be preserved between the *grounds* of justification and the *act* of justification, a distinction, it appears, that Horton's argument has not maintained clearly. In the light of Horton's conclusions, therefore, it is necessary to be clear as to the meaning of his statement that "the *act* of justification is logically prior to union,"[27] noting his reference to the *act*, and not to the *ground*, of justification. For what is relevant is not simply or only the ground on which God can and does have salvific dealings with man, but the actual process of those dealings in real historic time. The meaning of regeneration and justification as aspects of the application of redemption is thus raised for consideration.

Horton has argued challengingly and helpfully for what he refers to as a "forensic-covenantal ontology." He distances his argument from certain current erroneous claims for a "Neoplatonic participation" rather than a "covenantal participation" in Christ.[28] But in doing so he dissents from earlier Reformed formulations of the *ordo salutis*, notably on the point we have made regarding the comprehensive priority of union with Christ. The latter is acknowledged in Murray's comments that union with Christ is "a very broad and embracive subject. . . . [I]n its broader aspects it underlies every step of the application of redemption."[29] Horton's con-

---

23. Horton, *Covenant and Salvation*, 139.

24. Ibid., 143.

25. Ibid., 147.

26. Ibid., 203.

27. Ibid., 147, italics added.

28. Ibid., 153, 181.

29. Murray, *Redemption*, 201.

struction, to the contrary, is influenced by his apparent agreement with the claim that "regeneration . . . flows from justification as its consequence."[30] He states that the "initiating moment of new life [regeneration] . . . is the result of the justifying verdict that one receives through faith."[31]

That construction, in the context of Horton's attempt to effect a paradigm shift in Reformed theology, is justified, as he sees it, by what he imports from contemporary speech-act theory. In his discussion of "Speech-act theory and effectual calling," he concludes on that basis that "regeneration is not a direct and immediate act of God on the soul, but the perlocutionary effect of the illocutionary act pronounced by the Father in the Son through the Spirit."[32] In the terminology of speech-act theory an illocutionary act refers to what it is the speaker intends to convey by a statement he makes. It refers to the message, such as the intent to inform or persuade, for example, that the speaker sets out to communicate. The understanding of the statement in the mind of the hearer, on the other hand, or the "uptake" by the hearer, or what it is that actually functions in the hearer as the standard by which the meaning of what is said is to be measured and perhaps acted upon, is referred to as the perlocutionary response. In Horton's thought system he is leaving a wide opening for the Holy Spirit to apply to the human soul the meaning of what God has said. That applicatory, or perlocutionary, work of the Spirit is, in Horton's view, what is involved in, or amounts to, the regeneration of the sinner. In that way, Horton sees the perlocutionary work of regeneration following as a result of, and not as preceding, God's spoken act of justification. That, it is clear, is a deliberate inversion of the Reformed doctrine of the *ordo salutis* as it has been historically understood.

Regeneration, to the contrary, by reason of the endowments it conveys to the faculties of the soul, establishes the gift of faith as a capacity of exercise at the same time as it renews the soul in its union with Christ.[33] When, then, that newly endowed capacity of faith is exercised, the divine declarative act of justification follows. But when the *ordo salutis*, the ap-

---

30. Horton, op. cit., 202.

31. Ibid., 204.

32. Ibid., 220, 230.

33. That endowment of the faculties with new abilities and capacities and the creation of a new *habitus* in the soul do not necessarily raise the error of a participationist ontology from which Horton rightly dissents. Nor does it point to a "schizophrenic ontology" as Horton fears. See Horton, op. cit., 216.

plication of redemption, is then followed out in corresponding terms, the validity and usefulness of the Reformed construction as Berkhof, for example, has seen it become clear. Berkhof observes that "Even the very first blessing of the saving grace of God which we receive already presupposes a union with the Person of the Mediator."[34] He goes on to distinguish between God's work in the establishment of the union, the *unio mystica*, which "is effected by the Holy Spirit in a mysterious and supernatural way,"[35] and the believer's "subjective realization" of the union.[36] Noting the possible time differences involved, Berkhof concludes that "union with Him [Christ] logically precedes both regeneration and justification by faith, while yet, chronologically, the moment we are united with Christ is also the moment of our regeneration and justification." But Berkhof observes that the temporal relationship is further explained by the "reciprocal action" that is involved. "The initial act is that of Christ, who unites believers to himself by regenerating them and thus producing faith in them. On the other hand, the believer also unites himself to Christ by a conscious act of faith, and continues the union, under the influence of the Holy Spirit, by the constant exercise of faith."[37]

We note Berkhof's judicious separation of Christ's "*producing* faith" in the believer and the believer's "*act*" or "*exercise*" of faith. In short, as Berkhof concludes on this important relationship and "the mediation of the mystical union," "While the union is effected when the sinner is renewed by the operation of the Holy Spirit, he does not become cognizant of it and does not actively cultivate it until the conscious operation of faith begins."[38] Addressing "the subjective realization of the mystical union," Berkhof concludes that though we are joined to Christ as the branches are to the vine, "it is not correct to say that the mystical union is the fruit of man's believing acceptance of Christ."[39] For "Faith . . . a gift of God . . . enables us to appropriate on our part what is given unto us in Christ, and to enter ever-increasingly into conscious enjoyment of the blessed union

34. Berkhof, *Systematic Theology*, 447.

35. Idem.

36. Ibid., 450.

37. Idem.

38. Ibid., 452.

39. Ibid., 449.

with Christ, which is the source of all our spiritual riches."[40] The union with Christ of which we have spoken is not the result of faith in Christ; it is the reality from which faith in Christ emanates.

Before we comment on the relation of certain contemporary theologies to the questions we are addressing, it is necessary to refer to an important remaining implication of the believer's union with Christ. We have referred in the title of this chapter to the related doctrines of adoption and union with Christ. The Westminster Confession and the Savoy Declaration address in their parallel chapters 12 the doctrine of the believer's adoption into the family of God.[41] Leaving aside for the present the details of what are envisaged there as the blessings and privileges that connote membership of that family as children of God, it is rightly said that such believers are "sealed to the day of redemption, and inherit the promises, as heirs of everlasting salvation." It follows that it is as believers joined in union with Christ that all the privileges of adoption accrue to them. Again the reality of union with Christ spells out its comprehensive and determinative effects.

Let me put in another way what is involved in the relation between adoption and union with Christ. What, we may ask, provides to the repentant sinner his title to heaven? In the fundamental sense we have explored, the answer is that such a title is secured by the fact that God in his sovereign and inalienable purpose has established such a person in union with Christ. The title to heaven is secured, that is, by all that we have understood as God's eternally stated purpose to that effect, all of the aspects of which have been stated to be what they are by reason of God's directing them to the sinner "in Christ." But that purpose unfolds in the perfect realization in this world of the active and passive obedience of Christ. It is necessary to say, therefore, that in one of its aspects the title to heaven is secured by the active obedience of Christ. It is secured again by, or turns inevitably on, the passive obedience of Christ when he offered himself as the sinner's substitute in propitiating by his death the wrath of God against sin. But it is necessary to bring into relation in that way the significance of, first, the union with Christ in whom all aspects of salvation have been established, and secondly, the obedience of Christ that followed from that eternal ordination. What provides the title to heaven is

40. Berkhof, *Systematic Theology*, 449.

41. Similar statements are included also in the corresponding chapter 12 of the Second London (Baptist) Confession.

the fact that those who were chosen by God were, in very truth and with all its significance for salvation, united with Christ in all aspects of the work of redemption that he accomplished on their behalf.

THE RELEVANCE OF CONTEMPORARY THEOLOGIES

A question arises by implication from what has been said. If the believer who is now in union with Christ is, accordingly, an indefectible member of the family of God, and if he or she is, in fact, "sealed unto the day of redemption," how can it be contemplated that such a person may at last fail to achieve the eternal inheritance that is thereby promised? The prospect and the possibility of ultimate defection is held, however, by the doctrinal innovations we have mentioned: Shepherdism, the New Perspective on Paul (NPP), and the Federal Vision Theology (FV). It is precisely at that point that the inadmissibility of those theologies becomes most apparent. They argue for the possible defectibility from union with Christ of those who, purportedly, have been admitted to membership of the covenant kingdom of God. The expansive literature on those theologies makes it unnecessary to lay out at this time their detailed structure and claims. But while it is impossible in the present space to exhibit the content of those theologies at length, it is necessary to observe briefly the respects in which they impact our present concern.

It must be said, of course, that neither the NPP nor the FV theologies presents a monolithic construction that is agreed to by all those who make doctrinal statements consistent with one or the other of those systems' main propositions. But consider, for example, the claims made by the NPP as that addresses the doctrine of justification. Those claims follow from a radical reconstruction of what is to be understood as the covenant of God with his people.[42]

THE NEW PERSPECTIVE ON PAUL

Following the work of Krister Stendahl, which effectively set a new paradigm in Pauline studies, the most prominent and influential writer in what has become the NPP is undoubtedly E. P. Sanders.[43] Stendahl had argued

42. Expositions and critiques of what is referred to here in summary are available in the literature referred to in footnote 2.

43. Stendahl, "Paul Among Jews and Gentiles," in *Paul Among Jews and Gentiles*; E. P. Sanders, *Paul and Palestinian Judaism*.

that Paul's principal concern was to "defend the place of the Gentiles in the Kingdom—the task with which he was charged in his call."[44] He was not concerned with Luther's question, "How do I find a gracious God?"[45] but with "What are the ramifications of the Messiah's arrival for the relation between Jews and Gentiles?" Or, what is the "place of the Gentiles in the church and in the plan of God?"[46] When Paul speaks of justification he does not, according to Stendahl, contemplate what we understand as God's forensic declaration of imputed righteousness and the removal of the guilt of sin. For Paul's thought was not taken up, as Luther's had been, with the burdensome awareness of personal sin. For Stendahl, as N. T. Wright was to insist after him, righteousness, the "righteousness of God" for example, was not an abstract something that could be transferred to another person by imputation. The righteousness of God was God's vindication of his people, and that was extant by reason of God's gracious inclusion of them within the covenant. The "righteousness of God" is his covenantal faithfulness.[47]

Of immediate importance for our present study is the manner in which Sanders and Wright have expanded on these foundations. Sanders has emphasized that God by his grace established the Jews as his covenant people, though it is not clear what reasons are to be adduced for that initial covenantal establishment. But on that basis Sanders developed his concept of "covenantal nomism." He explains that in the following terms: "The 'pattern' or 'structure' of covenantal nomism is this: (1) God has chosen Israel and (2) given the law. That law implies both (3) God's promise to maintain the election and (4) the requirement to obey. (5) God rewards obedience and punishes transgression. (6) The law provides for means of atonement, and atonement results in (7) maintenance or re-establishment of the covenantal relationship. (8) All those who are maintained in the covenant by obedience, atonement and God's mercy belong to the

---

44. Stendahl, op. cit., 27.

45. Stendahl, "The Apostle Paul and the Introspective Conscience of the West," in op. cit., 83.

46. Ibid., 84.

47. Wright, *What Saint Paul Really Said*, 96. Wright argues that "If we use the language of the law court, it makes no sense whatever to say that the judge imputes, imparts, bequeaths, conveys or otherwise transfers his righteousness to either the plaintiff or the defendant. Righteousness is not an object, a substance or a gas which can be passed across the courtroom.... To imagine the defendant somehow receiving the judge's righteousness is simply a category mistake. That is not how the language works," ibid., 98.

group which will be saved. An important interpretation of the first and last points is that election and ultimately salvation are considered to be by God's mercy rather than human achievement."[48]

But it is to be noted that Sanders' construction of covenantal nomism places heavy weight on obedience to the law by those who are, assumedly, already within the covenant. Sanders explains further that "Briefly put, covenantal nomism is the view that one's place in God's plan is established on the basis of the covenant and that the covenant requires as the proper response of man his obedience to its commandments, while providing means of atonement for transgression."[49] But as noted below, the concept of atonement is variously interpreted.[50] This has led to the conclusion that one "gets in" the covenantal relation by the electing grace of God, and one "stays in," or "maintains" the covenantal relation, by works of obedience and repentance. It is clear that all of this is widely distanced from what we have seen as the indefectibility of those who have been chosen as God's covenantal people by reason of their established union with Christ. A sound interpretation of the biblical data that bear on adoption and union with Christ is not admitted in the scheme of things the NPP proposes.

We have referred to the work of N. T. Wright whose extensive and popular writings have had heavy influence on the dissemination of the NPP agenda. In addition to what we have noted as his dismissal of the doctrine and the fact of the imputation of Christ's righteousness, one of Wright's principal contributions relevant to our present concern is his expansion of the notion of covenantal membership. For that purpose Wright places emphasis on what he conceives of as the Lordship of Christ. In his doing so, we see a decided emphasis on the *Person* of Christ, his status as Lord, and not on the *work* of Christ. The important fact, as Ligon Duncan has captured the sense of Wright's claim at this point, is that "Jesus is Lord,"

---

48. Sanders, *Paul and Palestinian Judaism*, 422.

49. Ibid., 75. It is important to understand Sanders' notion of "atonement" at this stage. If one should sin, it is argued, an atonement was provided in the structure of the legal administration of the covenant. One could thereby "stay in" the covenant. God's mercy predominates over his justice. "The Rabbis never said that God is merciful in such a way as to remove the necessity of obeying him, but they did think that God was merciful toward those who basically intended to obey, even though their performance might have been a long way from perfect." *Paul and Palestinian Judaism*, 125. The means of atonement within the covenantal structure were repentance, the Old Testament sacrifices, suffering, and the death of the repentant individual. Sanders, op. cit., 158–59, 178.

50. Ibid.

not that "Jesus died for your sin."[51] That is a reflection again of Sanders' conclusion that "Christ came to be lord of all [but] men were under a different lordship. . . . Man's problem is not being under Christ's lordship. Since this is the real problematic, the traditional language of repentance and forgiveness is almost entirely missing [from Paul's writing]."[52] "Christ's lordship . . . this is [Paul's] gospel."[53] And following that emphasis, Wright stresses the lordship of Christ as a focal point of Christian belief. One critic observes that in doing so he "purges soteriological categories from Pauline theological reflection."[54] For Wright, people become Christian because "they come to believe the message; they join the Christian community through baptism, and begin to share in its common life and its common way of life. That is how people come into relationship with the living God."[55] "Believing in Jesus—believing that Jesus is Lord, and the [sic] God raised him from the dead—is what counts."[56] One may even be "justified without knowing it."[57]

The threads of the NPP argument are brought explicitly to prominence by Wright again when he concludes that "Justification . . . is not a matter of *how someone enters the community of the true people of God*, but of *how you tell who belongs to that community*, not least in the period of time before the eschatological event itself, when the matter will become public knowledge."[58] And "'the gospel' is not an account of how people get saved. It is . . . the proclamation of the lordship of Jesus Christ. . . . Let us be quite clear. 'The gospel' is the announcement of Jesus' lordship, which works with power to bring people into the family of Abraham, now redefined around Jesus Christ and characterized solely by faith in him. 'Justification' is the doctrine which insists that all those who have this faith belong as full members of this family, on this basis and no other."[59]

51. See Duncan's essay, "The Attraction of the New Perspective(s) on Paul."

52. Sanders, *Paul and Palestinian Judaism*, 500.

53. Ibid., 445–46.

54. Waters, *Justification and the New Perspective on Paul*, 201. See also ibid., x.

55. Wright, *What Saint Paul Really Said*, 116–17. It will be seen below that Wright's statement, "they join the Christian community through baptism," is fundamental in a precise sense and with a very special meaning to the agenda of the Federal Vision theology.

56. Ibid., 159.

57. Idem.

58. Ibid., 119.

59. Ibid., 133. See also ibid., 45, 60, 118.

The "gospel," as Wright sees it, is not "something that in older theology would be called an *ordo salutis*, an order of salvation."[60]

It might be noted at this point that Gaffin has responded to this emphasis of Wright by observing that "Wright is emphatic that Jesus is Lord, but much less clear about how he is Savior. His presentation of Paul's gospel is at least open to being construed as follows: it's not that Jesus, because he's my Savior, is my Lord; rather, as he's my Lord, he's my Savior—in the sense that my salvation consists in my continuing allegiance to Jesus as Lord. The danger that this in its own way opens the door to moralism is hardly imaginary."[61]

The NPP agenda, as we have inspected it briefly in the works of Sanders and Wright, contains an idiosyncratic construction of God's covenant and the possibility of defectible membership of it. Concentrating as it does on a somewhat indiscriminate claim to Christ's lordship, it fails to grasp the true meaning of entrance to life in Christ by justification and the imputation of his righteousness, and it fails to recognize, as a result, the real implications for the Christian life of union with Christ. In doing so, the NPP brings together in a theory of relationship to Christ a set of concepts that differ vastly from what we have seen as the meaning and import of the biblical data that bear on the believer's union with Christ. The NPP failure to understand what the biblical doctrines of adoption and union with Christ mean and entail, it can be repeated, is the point at which the NPP scheme is biblically unsustainable.

THE FEDERAL VISION THEOLOGY

It is again a particular and a less than biblical understanding of God's covenant with his people that vitiates the Federal Vision theological agenda. The conception of the covenant is accompanied there also by the notion that one who is, purportedly, in full union with Christ may fall away and be eternally lost. Admittedly, as can be observed from a more extensive study of the FV literature than can be reported at this time, some of its authors have claimed that the statement just made misrepresents their true position. But as further comments will show, it is not thought that such a counterclaim is sustainable.

---

60. Ibid., 40–41.

61. Gaffin, "Paul the Theologian," 125.

The FV theology received an initial impulse from the earlier work of Norman Shepherd who, writing in the 1970s while a member of the faculty of Westminster Theological Seminary, proposed a doctrine that amounted to justification by faith plus works. In his subsequent book, *The Call of Grace*, Shepherd refers to the "covenantal righteousness of Christ," and observing that "His was a living, active, and obedient faith" he continues, "Just as Jesus was faithful in order to *guarantee* the blessing, so his followers must be faithful in order to *inherit* the blessing."[62] That accords with Shepherd's frequent statement that justification is by "obedient faith," where the insertion of the adjective conjures the notion that justification will be finally established by the divine declaration to that effect at the day of judgment.[63] The strength of that supposed datum in Shepherd's scheme is to be seen in the light of his argument that an individual's continued obedience "is necessary to his continuing in a state of justification."[64] Shepherd continues: "The righteousness of Jesus Christ ever remains the exclusive ground of the believer's justification, but *the personal godliness of the believer is also necessary* for his justification in the judgment of the last day. . . . *[G]ood works . . .* though not the ground [of the believer's] justification, *are nevertheless necessary for justification.*"[65] In short, for Shepherd again the person who is joined to Christ in a state of having been justified is, nevertheless, defectible. That is, one can lose his justification.[66]

It is explicit in Shepherd's claims that the apparent difference between Paul and James on the matter of faith and works is to be resolved by the recognition that both are speaking, in their respective contexts, of forensic justification. That itself dissents from the traditional Reformed understanding that whereas Paul speaks of forensic justification, James is concerned with demonstrative justification. In short, Shepherd's doctrine fails to grasp the once-for-all effectiveness of God's declarative-forensic-judicial statement of justification, clearly grounded in the imputation of the righteousness of

62. Shepherd, *Call of Grace*, 19. See the insightful comment in Eveson, *The Great Exchange*, 170–71.

63. See Shepherd, *Call of Grace*, 50: "A living, active, and abiding faith is the way in which the believer enters into eternal life," and ibid., 51: "eternal life . . . we enter into it by way of a living, active, and obedient faith."

64. Shepherd, *Thirty-Four Theses*, Thesis 21. See also the discussion of Shepherd's theses in Robertson, *Current Justification Controversy*, 34–35 et passim.

65. Shepherd, Theses 22, 23, italics added.

66. See Shepherd, Thesis 21.

Christ, at the point of the sinner's exercise of faith and trust in Christ as Savior. Shepherd argues that it is a mistake to "make good works a supplement to salvation or simply the *evidence* of salvation .... According to the Great Commission, however, they belong to the *essence* of salvation."[67]

Shepherd's alignment with the FV doctrines is pointedly clear in his understanding of the place and significance of baptism as a covenantal ordinance. "Baptism," he claims, "the sign and seal of the covenant, marks the point of conversion. Baptism is the moment when we see the transition from death to life and the person is saved."[68] That motif has been taken up by FV authors and is central to their particular construction of the covenant and individual membership within it.

A number of related concepts coalesce to determine the FV claims at this point. First, following the lead of Shepherd, the matter of God's election is seen through the lens of the covenant and needs to be understood from the perspective that the covenant provides. (When Shepherd makes that claim, for example, he states: "Instead of looking at covenant from the perspective of regeneration, we ought to look at regeneration from the perspective of covenant,"[69] and in that context he argues, as stated above, that "When that happens, baptism . . . marks the point of conversion."); second, some FV authors (with Shepherd) reject the doctrine of the covenant of works and speak of a monocovenantal conception of God's relation with his people (implying, in its rejection of the distinctions between the covenant of works and the covenant of grace, that obedience as the way of covenant blessing is the same in the pre-redemptive and the redemptive covenants); third, the concept of covenant itself is understood to be a matter of relationship, and that relationship, it is generally said, is to be understood in objective terms and one enters that objective covenant relation at the point of baptism. (This again follows Shepherd who defines a covenant as "a divinely established relationship of union and communion between God and his people."[70] The covenant is frequently said to be "an objective relationship independent of the covenant member's subjective considerations of the strength or nature of his membership."[71]); fourth, insisting on the objectivity of the covenant,

---

67. Shepherd, *Call of Grace*, 104, italics added.

68. Ibid., 94.

69. Idem.

70. Ibid., 12.

71. Waters, *Federal Vision*, 14. See references cited there.

the concept is held of undifferentiated covenant membership that leads to the admissibility, even the necessity as some FV authors see it, of paedo-communion; fifth, the conclusion follows that there is a general rejection of the distinction between, and the relation between, the church in its visible and its invisible aspects.[72]

It will throw light on these related issues to observe further the respects in which the objective entry to the covenant relation via the rite of baptism determines the FV understanding of union with Christ and the possibility of defection from that status. Douglas Wilson, for example, a prominent FV advocate, argues that "baptism in water is objective, and it establishes an objective covenant relation with the Lord of the covenant, Jesus Christ."[73] Or again, "Baptism is covenantally efficacious. It brings every person baptized into an objective and living relationship with Christ, whether the baptized person is elect or reprobate. Baptism is always to be taken by the one baptized as a sign and seal of his ingrafting into Christ."[74] Wilson continues at that point to say that "If the person is reprobate, he will be cut out of the vine, and if he is elect, he cannot be cut out." But it is important to recognize that in Wilson's conception, as in that of the FV more generally, the "cutting out of the vine" potentially occurs to those who have already been "ingrafted into Christ." Waters captures the essence and implication of Wilson's claims when he comments, "We must read Wilson's statements to the effect that one ought to regard an individual who is seriously defective in doctrine . . . as a 'fellow Christian,' provided that such a one is 'lawfully baptized in the name of the Father, Son, and Holy Ghost.'"[75] In short, by and in virtue of his baptism one is a Christian in union with Christ, but from that union he or she is potentially defectible. We have again, that is, the FV failure to admit the meaning of union with Christ in its full and biblically stated sense. That is the mark of the unsustainability of the FV theology.

The point we have just made is reinforced by what the FV proponents have to say explicitly of one's union with Christ. Steve Wilkins, for example, states that "baptism *unites us to Christ* and his church and thus gives us new life. . . . Christ's baptism meant that the old things were

---

72. See the summary and critique in Waters, ibid., passim.

73. Wilson, *"Reformed" is not Enough*, 99. cited in Waters, *Federal Vision*, 206.

74. Wilson, "A Short Collection of Credos: On Baptism" cited in Waters, *Federal Vision*, 209.

75. Waters, *Federal Vision*, 147.

passed, the sin and the curse of the law had passed away and all things had become new. The same is true for all who are baptized."[76] If it is asked what, precisely, Wilkins has in view in his concept of covenantal union that baptism effects, he replies, "at baptism you are clothed with Christ. Union with Christ is a real, vital blessed union."[77] It is true that Wilkins at that point appears to endeavor to distinguish "real" from covenantal union, but the lack of clarity that exists fails to rescue his statement, along with similar counterclaims by FV authors, from the firm impression that it is defectibility from an established and spiritually substantial union with Christ that is inherent in their scheme of things. Indeed, Wilkins is explicit in arguing, with Shepherd, that "baptism (not regeneration)" is "the time of transition from unbelief to faith, from death to life, from the world to the kingdom of heaven."[78]

Another FV proponent, Rich Lusk, submits a similar claim in his statement that "baptism unites us to Christ.... At the very least ... baptism puts the one baptized into a state of salvation. It grafts us into Christ's body that we may share his life ... [baptism] is the instrumental means of union with Christ."[79] But it is not necessary to multiply citations further. Suffice it to say that the FV theologians heavily emphasize union with Christ, but, as has been recognized in different contexts, it would be a misrepresentation to conclude that what they hold in view in that concept is biblically supportable or accords with the traditional Reformed, and historically held, doctrinal conclusions.

A PARADIGM SHIFT IN REFORMED THEOLOGY

On a somewhat different level the doctrine of the believer's union with Christ has also formed the basis of the long-established work of Richard Gaffin. Gaffin has enthusiastically and publicly defended the writing of Norman Shepherd and has commended the latter's *The Call of Grace*, to which we have already referred, as a "lucid and highly readable study that provides valuable instruction.... [It] should benefit anyone concerned about

---

76. Wilkins, "The Legacy of the Half-Way Covenant," cited in Waters, *Federal Vision,* 140, italics added.

77. Wilkins, op. cit., cited in Waters, *Federal Vision,* 232.

78. Wilkins, "Apostasy and the Covenant (II)," cited in Waters, *Federal Vision,* 237.

79. Rich Lusk, "Some Thoughts on the Means of Grace," cited in Waters, *Federal Vision,* 216, 359.

biblical growth in Christian life and witness."[80] While it is not necessary, or not even necessarily appropriate, to saddle Gaffin with all of Shepherd's doctrinal defects, it is true that Gaffin comes into confluence with the Federal Vision theology in his holding to a particular view of the doctrinal significance of the believer's union with Christ. Notwithstanding what we noticed earlier as Gaffin's objection to Wright's emphasis on the lordship of Christ, his own work points noticeably in that direction. For taking up the cognate issues of justification and union with Christ, Gaffin's most fundamental doctrinal proposition, as was noted in an earlier chapter, is that "Not justification by faith but union with the resurrected Christ by faith (of which union, to be sure, the justifying aspect stands out most prominently) is the central motif of Paul's applied soteriology."[81] While it is not possible to agree with Gaffin's apparent move in allowing the truth of our union with Christ to swallow up all other soteriological perspectives, and while we are sensitive, as we have shown, to the importance of the fact and the doctrine of our union with Christ, it is necessary to look more closely at what Gaffin discloses as the meaning of the terms he employs.

As Gaffin understands and presents it, the believer's redemption, justification, adoption, and sanctification are what they are because of the respects in which he shares in, and partakes of, those blessings as they exist in Christ. They so exist because of, and by virtue of, Christ's resurrection. "The subjectively transforming elements of saving experience," he says, "are aspects of having been raised with Christ . . . forensic elements are likewise facets of being joined to the resurrected Christ. Galatians 3:26f, makes clear that the adoption in Christ received through faith derives from being baptized into Christ . . . justification depends not simply on an action in the past experience of the believer but on his present relation to the person of the resurrected Christ."[82] Gaffin concludes further, again reflecting shades of Shepherd's doctrinal system, that "the justification, adoption, sanctification, and glorification of the believer are future as well as present."[83] Gaffin expands his meaning at that point by observing, however, in what is no doubt a divergence from Shepherd, that "believers are already justified—by

80. Gaffin, commendation of Shepherd, *Call of Grace*, back cover.

81. Gaffin, *Resurrection and Redemption*, 132. See also the same author's *"By Faith, Not By Sight,"* 43.

82. Gaffin, *Resurrection and Redemption*, 132–33.

83. Ibid., 133.

faith. But they are yet to be justified—by sight."[84] But the question arises of what precisely is involved in Gaffin's claim at that point.

Gaffin maintains his concentration on the believer's union with Christ in the sense we have noted in his work because, as he argues, "That union also has judicial or forensic significance, *as does Christ's own resurrection.*"[85] By that he means that "Christ's resurrection is his own justification,"[86] and "the resurrection is . . . Christ's justification or the point of entering into a state of being justified."[87] The sense in which union with Christ thus becomes the central coordinating motif in Gaffin's theology follows from his references to "The resurrection as the redemption of Christ,"[88] and similarly, "the resurrection of Jesus is his *adoption,*"[89] "Jesus' resurrection is his justification,"[90] and "Christ's resurrection [is] his sanctification."[91]

That line of doctrinal development, we have noted, sees the individual believer's justification, adoption, and sanctification as coming to effect and being what they are because at relevant levels the believer partakes of, or shares in, the redemption, justification, adoption, and sanctification that Christ achieved for himself, and by his doing so achieved for those who are joined in union to him. In that respect Gaffin's conclusion is worthy of recall: "[W]hat characterizes the redemption of Christ holds true for the redemption of the believer. As the justification, adoption, sanctification, and glorification of the former take place by and at his resurrection, so the justification, adoption, sanctification, and glorification of the latter take place in his having been raised with Christ, that is, in his having been united with Christ as resurrected. This means, then, that, despite a surface appearance to the contrary, Paul does not view the justification, adoption, sanctification, and glorification of the believer as separate, distinct acts but as different facets or aspects of the *one act* of incorporation with the resurrected Christ"[92]

84. Gaffin, *"By Faith, Not By Sight,"* 88.

85. Ibid., 84, italics added.

86. Idem.

87. Gaffin, *Resurrection and Redemption,* 121. Gaffin here follows closely the work of Vos, who speaks of "the justification of Christ," *Pauline Eschatology,* 151.

88. Gaffin, *Resurrection and Redemption,* 114.

89. Ibid., 118.

90. Ibid., 123.

91. Ibid., 124.

92. Gaffin, *Resurrection and Redemption,* 130–31.

It is beyond our present objective to provide a full critique of Gaffin's doctrinal system which, he acknowledges, is developed from the redemptive-historical orientation in the work of Geerhardus Vos and Herman Ridderbos.[93] Gaffin's attempt to effect a paradigm shift in Reformed theology by his concentration on *historia salutis* and his diminution of the traditional *ordo salutis* cannot be judged an unqualified success. For a sound and necessary recognition of *historia salutis* does not require the conclusion Gaffin reaches in his concentration on the resurrection of Christ as being Christ's own redemption. His argument, notwithstanding the nuances with which he labors, leaves it doubtful that adequate account has been taken of the Person and work of the Redeemer. For given our Lord's divine Personhood, into union with which he has taken a sinless human nature, the focus of our thought might more properly fall, not on a supposition that Christ stood in need of redemption, but on his sinless substitution for sinners in his redemptive accomplishment. It is a misstep in Reformed theology to argue, as Gaffin does, for Christ's own personal redemption, justification, adoption, and sanctification.

Gaffin's theological orientation misconstrues the *way* of salvation, for salvation turns, in his system, not on the sinner's exercise of faith and repentance at the cross of Christ at a point in real time, but on, as he emphasizes, an existential union with Christ.[94] The object of the sinner's faith is not, in Gaffin's soteriology, Christ in his substitutionary work on the cross when he died in the sinner's place. Gaffin's particular construction of a *historia salutis* and the diminution of the *ordo salutis* avoids an adequate presentation of the manner in which the forensic acts of God are applied to the believer in real historic time. He argues, moreover, that "Paul views them [justification etc.] not as distinct acts but as distinct aspects of a single act ['union with the resurrected Christ by faith']," so that "what need is there for the other acts?"[95]

Gaffin's apparent collapsing of the benefits of Christ's redemption into union with him in the manner he has proposed, giving rise as it does to the danger of subjugating the forensic to the relational and providing a basis for certain FV theses, is echoed in the work of the FV author, Rich Lusk. Harking back to what we observed in our discussion of the

93. See the bibliography in Ibid., 145–46.

94. See the comments in Elliott, *Christianity and Neo-Liberalism*, 150, 160.

95. Gaffin, *Resurrection and Redemption,* 138–39. See also Ibid., 132.

NPP, Lusk states that "[J]ustification requires no transfer or imputation of anything. It does not force us to reify 'righteousness' into something that can be shuffled around in heavenly accounting books. Rather, because I am in the Righteous One and the Vindicated One, I am righteous and vindicated. My in-Christ-ness makes imputation redundant. I do not need the moral content of his life of righteousness transferred to me; *what I need is a share in the forensic verdict passed over him at the resurrection.* Union with Christ is therefore the key."[96] Gaffin's doctrinal construction is echoed in the italicized conclusion in Lusk's statement.

To conceive of the several elements of the believer's state of salvation in the manner Gaffin proposes distances one from what might be taken as the previously established norm of Reformed thought.[97] For to redefine regeneration, justification, adoption, and sanctification in the participatory sense of union with Christ in the manner Gaffin has done vacates the doctrines of their classically held and biblically sustainable meaning. Gaffin's proposals imply a diminution, if not an abandonment, of what Reformed theology has held under the rubric of the *ordo salutis*. His doctrinal propositions detract from, if not eliminate, justification and sanctification as spoken and operative acts of God. For purposes of our present study, the meaning and significance of the believer's union with Christ are explicable on different grounds from what Gaffin, as well as the NPP and FV theologies, has proposed.

ADOPTION AND UNION WITH CHRIST AND THE CHRISTIAN LIFE

Our task at this stage is twofold. We shall extract from our earlier statements of adoption and union with Christ what it is that differentiates those blessings from the claims that are made by certain contemporary theologies; and with our doctrinal stance in hand we shall reflect more deeply on the implied benefits they project for the Christian life and walk.

First, we hold to two propositions. In the first place we acknowledge what Reformed theology has traditionally understood as the twofold significance and relevance of the believer's union with Christ. That union

---

96. Lusk, "A response to 'The Biblical Plan of Salvation'," in *The Auburn Avenue Theology*, 142, cited in Orthodox Presbyterian Church, *Justification: Report*, 145, italics added.

97. Gaffin explicitly notes that the perspective his work adopts represents "a difference in accent from what has largely been true beginning with the Reformation," *"By Faith, Not by Sight,"* 24.

was established in the eternal counsel of God, following which God has had dealings with us only in his Son. That is true in the sense that our very creation was entrusted to the Son (John 1:3; Col. 1:16); and in the theophanic appearance of the Son, God walked with our first parents in the garden in the cool of the day (Gen. 3:8). Subsequent such appearances are spread throughout the pages of Old Testament history. Then in the fullness of time God the Son, the Second Person of the Godhead, came into this world as Jesus Christ to be man for our redemption and to identify himself with us in all aspects of his accomplishment of that redemption. Because God, in the eternal decree of redemption, looked on us as the chosen subjects of that decree, he has always seen us in his Son. It has never been the case that God has regarded us distinct from, or as separate from, his own Son. That is the sense in which whatever is to be said regarding our redemption and eternal security is to be said within the context of our union with Christ. God has never contemplated us apart from Christ.

Secondly, we not only hold in that manner to our union with Christ as an all- determining environment of God's relation with us, but we trace out at the same time the respects in which that union has given rise to God's actions in real time that structure the outcomes necessary for our redemption. We hold, that is, that regeneration, or more comprehensively God's effectual calling, is an act of God that results in the awareness and realization that we are united to Christ. We hold that justification and adoption are acts of God's free grace, and that sanctification is an actual and progressive work of God's grace that conforms the believer to the holiness of Christ. With those conclusions in hand, our doctrine is differentiated from modern alternatives in that we hold the believer's union with Christ, in the context of God's eternal covenant of grace, to be indissoluble. The individual now joined in union with Christ is indefectible. Though remnants of sin remain, and though the individual's life-journey may have its interruptions and not exhibit a steady upward incline to glory, we have it on the authority of our Lord himself that nothing will pluck us out of his hand (John 10:28). We hold to the historic actions of God in time that bring the content of God's decrees and purposes to temporal effect. And we hold to the real and temporal awareness within the individual consciousness of God's effectual working out of his designs for our salvation.

What, then, is to be said of the blessings and benefits that accrue, as a result, to the believer? First, we hold to the fact that adoption into the family of God is "an act of God's free grace" that gives us "a right to all the privileges of the sons of God,"[98] and we see, and we find relief in the fact, that adoption is God's forensic act. As justification is a declarative-forensic act and statement of God, so again is adoption. Adoption is a once-for-all act and decision of God that cannot be either repeated or annulled. It is God's legally declaring us a member of his family. The high status that is thus accorded us clarifies the privileges that lie ahead, and it motivates our sense of responsibility to live, by God's grace, worthy of them.

That being so, the imperatives that bear on the Christian life follow from the twofold privileged status the Christian now enjoys. First, as has been said, he has been legally adopted into a new family under the presidency of a new Fatherhood. But that is not the end of what is to be said. Not only are we adopted into the family, but we have actually been joined in a spiritual and substantial union with the Head of the family. We are now joined to Christ in all of the ways we have explored and, as has been said, we are thereby joined in union with the triune Persons of the Godhead. The realization of those two aspects of our privileged status is what, from that time on, must determine the character and quality of our life in this world. We may work out some of the detailed implications in the following way.

In our doctrinal statement we have observed the association that exists between God's endowment of the grace of regeneration and the fact and consciousness of the believer's union with Christ. It is true that regeneration involves and carries with it the endowment of faith, by the exercise of which the sinner turns to Christ. It may well be said that an aspect of simultaneity exists between faith and union with Christ. But at that point it is necessary to differentiate between the endowment of faith as a capacity of soul that is conveyed to the sinner in his regeneration on the one hand, and, on the other hand, the actual exercise of that capacity of faith by the sinner when he comes to belief in Christ. That implies that one's union with Christ is antecedent to the exercise of faith. And the error is exposed of those who claim, though they are undoubtedly speaking too loosely in doing so, that it is by faith that union with Christ

---

98. Westminster Shorter Catechism, Question 34.

is established. Union with Christ is antecedent to, not the consequent of, the exercise of faith.

We say we are joined in union to Christ. But who is the Christ with whom that union exists? It is, as the biblical data declare copiously, the incarnate Christ. That is the reality to be grasped. The Second Person of the Godhead came into this world, born of a woman, made under the law, taking to himself in union with his divine nature a perfect human nature, that he might be like us in order to redeem us from the curse of sin. We shun all suggestions of Gnosticism, Docetism, and notions of phantom bodies and suggestions that the spiritual and the material could not come into true union. It is not a work of supererogation to repeat and to insist on the point that we are redeemed by, and we now live in union with, Christ in his incarnate personhood. We are joined in spiritual union with our Lord who now sits in the heavens in his human nature, still and for ever joined to his divine nature, discharging his heavenly high priestly office on our behalf. In his high priestly office he intercedes for us, and because he too is human he knows us and sympathizes with us in all of the aspects and developments of our life-journey until we come to him in the last great day.

Union with Christ, then, makes imperative the pursuit of the Christian believer's personal holiness. In the simplest of terms, the one who is conscious of the high privilege that has been accorded him can have no higher ambition than to be like his Savior. It is not necessary to expand at this point all that can be said of the process of the Christian's sanctification as the righteousness of Christ is progressively formed in him. It is true that there will be no progress in sanctification unless and until there is progress in the mortification of sin. That is implicit in the catechetical statement that "Sanctification is the work of God's free grace, whereby we are renewed in the whole man after the image of God, and are enabled more and more to die unto sin, and live unto righteousness."[99] But setting aside for the present the details of what it is important to consider as the process of sanctification, let us raise, rather, the following questions in the light of what has been said regarding our adoption and union with Christ.

What is our vision of Christ, now as we see him by faith, as he ministers to us by his Spirit, as he prepares before us the very way in which we walk, and as he calls us to respond to his redemptive love for us? Do

99. Westminster Shorter Catechism, Question 35.

we see him as the prophet of old described him, "despised and rejected of men," in whom there is "no form nor comeliness; and when we see him there is no beauty that we should desire him"? (Isa. 53:2–3). Or do we see him as did the spouse in Solomon's Song, as "altogether lovely"? (Song 5:16). Is there any excitement of heart as we hear him say, "I stand at the door and knock; if any man hear my voice, and open the door, I will come in to him, and will sup with him, and he with me"? (Rev. 3:20). Are our ears attuned to his gracious voice? Is the moment of his presence with us better than life itself?

We have heard of his compassion for the disadvantaged and disabled, his giving hearing to the deaf, sight to the blind, and even life to the dead. We have heard of his identification with the sorrows of humanity he came to save. We have learned that he was so sensitive to the needs of a poor sinner that he was conscious of virtue having gone out of him at even the touch of the hem of his garment. We have seen it well-attested that never was there a man in this world who spoke as he did. He had in his Person power and authority to command devils, to still an angry sea, to direct his disciples to where they could find a draft of fish, and we have learned of his power to defeat the devil when he was tempted in all points like as we are. We know these things, but have we responded to his word when he tells us he directs the same compassion, grace, and power to us his people in our necessities?

We have heard it said that we have a high priest who is "touched with the feeling of our infirmities [and who] was in all points tempted like as we are," and that we may therefore "come boldly unto the throne of grace, that we may obtain mercy, and find grace to help in time of need." (Heb. 4:15–16). But do we live in a manner that suggests we believe what we have heard? We have heard that he said, "Come unto me, all ye that labour and are heavy laden, and I will give you rest" (Matt. 11:28). But has that gracious invitation registered with us in such a way that we believe and know that it is for us?

The Scriptures have told us that the Christ to whom we are joined in a union that nothing can destroy is the sinless Son of God, and that he waits patiently to form his holiness within us. The prospect seems, somehow, too high for us. The weakness of flesh rebels. And in the contemplation of his presence we are conscious of our sin and unworthiness. Conscience touched by the grace of God tells us we cannot continue in sin that grace may abound (Rom. 6:1). In our best moments of self-realization we have hated sin. But we know that if we told ourselves we had no sin we should lie (I John 1:8). But have we known the calming intensity of the truth that if we confess our sin the Christ whose we are and to whom we are joined will forgive our sin and cleanse us from all unrighteousness (1 John 1:9)? We have learned a good deal of the truth of the doctrines of the grace of God so freely directed to our eternal benefit in Christ. But has our complacency and the ordinary carelessness of life been shattered by the simple but life-determining truth that Christ died for sinners? Why, then, does not our sin, and the burning consciousness of sin, drive us again to Christ and the relief that abounds freely only in him?

We have known the peace of soul when, in our best moments, we have realized that now we are no longer trapped in the realm of sin, condemnation, and death, but that by the grace of God set forth in Christ we have been "translated . . . into the kingdom of his dear Son" (Col. 1:13), to the realm of righteousness, justification, and life. But the pressure of everyday, as the clamor of the world presses upon us, too frequently and too much diverts us from what we know is the only true source of life. Too often we are ashamed because we have too easily accommodated the things and patterns and idioms of the world. We lament our unworthiness. But have we been careful to remember that our gracious Lord, who did not save us for our worthiness, will not leave us or forsake us for our unworthiness? Have we remembered that he knows our frame, he sees our walk in all its stumbling uncertainties, and yet, because he has taken us into that indissoluble union with himself, he still and for ever holds out his hand of rescue and carefully draws us to himself again? Too often we are not numbered among the ninety-nine. But our Lord's concern is rich in the care he has for the sheep that has wandered. Do we hear his call again? He still says, "Come unto me."

But in our walk in what may be often a vale of tears, anxiety, and alarm at the arrows that we interpret as misfortune, forgetting that all things are under the good and providential hand of our Savior, we are tempted to wonder whether our very standing in grace is what we have thought it to be. Perhaps we have misunderstood. Perhaps, after all, we have not been numbered among those whom Christ died to redeem. The doctrine, as that is cognizable in propositional terms, is well understood, but perhaps our faith has not been as true or as large or as sound as we thought it to be, and perhaps we have even misled ourselves into a false assumption of security. If we were not truly in such a condition, surely our faculties of soul, our mind and heart and conscience, would not be disturbed as now they are.

If such a state, with its fears and turmoiled and clamoring passions, rises, have we remembered that even there our Lord to whom we are joined knows all about us? Have we paused in our self-flagellation to remember that he waits for us to come to him again; or better, that he will come again by his Spirit with the soothing balm of his grace, the assurance of his love for his saints? Satan condemns us. Our own hearts condemn us. But Christ has died for us and we have it on the basis of his unarguable promise that he will, with it all, not fail to conduct us to the glory that he has prepared and promised we shall share with him. Did he not say that he was going to prepare a place for us (John 14:3)? Do we not have it on the authority of his word that "he which hath begun a good work in you will perform [perfect] it until the day of Jesus Christ" (Phil 1:6)?

Away, then, with doubt and discouragement. Away with the thought that demeans the very grace that has saved us. For it is not the largeness or what we conjure as the soundness of our faith that saves us. It is Christ in his Person and his substitutionary redemptive work that saves us. Let us look away from our own poor selves and the world that is seemingly too much with us in this short, uncertain life and earthly pilgrimage, and let us look to the Christ whose we are, and to the security we have because, as we have now reflected upon it at length, we are joined to him in a vital and indissoluble union.

8

The Scope of Salvation

IN HIS FIRST LETTER to the Corinthians the apostle Paul captures in a single and comprehensive sentence the scope of salvation that God has provided in Christ. "Of him [God] are ye in Christ Jesus, who of [or by] God is made unto us wisdom, and righteousness, and sanctification, and redemption" (1 Cor. 1:30). Christ is made to us wisdom against our ignorance, righteousness against our guilt, sanctification against pollution, and redemption against the misery in which we should otherwise have been left.[1] The grace of God is addressed to the sinner's guilt, and the mercy of God is addressed to his misery. The apostolic statement brings that to emphasis by focusing his thought on the sovereignty of God in salvation. Our salvation, the apostle says, is all of grace. "By grace are ye saved through faith; and that not of yourselves; it is the gift of God" (Eph. 2:8). And in the total scope of salvation all the benefits of redemption accrue to the sinner by virtue of his union with Christ. The sinner who is now the beneficiary of a transition from wrath to grace was identified with Christ in his full obedience, in all that Christ did for the sinner's salvation.

The focus of this chapter is the Christian's development in sanctification. That turns on an understanding of the pollution of sin against which progress in holiness is to be made. It was observed in a previous chapter that while the unregenerate person will know nothing of the true meaning of sin until he has seen something of the holiness of God, the regenerate individual will progress in holiness only as he has a deepen-

1. The present writer well remembers the impact that the opposing elements included in that sentence made when they were stated in that form by Dr. Martyn Lloyd-Jones, one of the foremost preachers of the twentieth century, in Westminster Chapel, London, England, during the height of his ministry. It is worthy of note that the same statement had been made previously by the Puritan, John Flavel, in his sermon on 1 Corinthians 1:30, the first in his series on "The Method of Grace in the Gospel Redemption," reprinted in Flavel, *Works*, vol. 2, 15–33. See page 16.

ing understanding of the meaning of sin. By that is meant the pollution that clings to him by reason of the state in which the grace of God finds him. The redemptive work of Christ rescues the sinner from the guilt, the power, and the pollution of sin. And the saving work of Christ provides the motivation to the mortification of sin in the believer's life without which sanctification cannot proceed. "Work out your own salvation," is the apostolic imperative, "for it is God which worketh in you both to will and to do of his good pleasure" (Phil. 2:12–13).

Christ, the Corinthian text says, is our sanctification. To understand what is involved we recall that theologians have been accustomed to speak of the "ontological trinity" of the Godhead, intending thereby to refer to God in his essence and being as existing in three Persons, "the same in substance," as the catechism says, "equal in power and glory."[2] Then when attention is focused on the works of God, particularly as we have before us now the work of redemption, they have spoken of the "economic trinity." The term "economic" is taken to refer to the distribution among the Persons of the Godhead of offices or functions relating to the full accomplishment of the work designed. From among fallen humanity made up of Adam and all his posterity God the Father chose to eternal salvation those whom he gave to his Son to redeem (John 17:6). It was the office of God the Son to come into the world, to assume human nature into union with his divine nature, and to provide the work of obedience and death necessary to save his people. The Holy Spirit undertook to apply to those whom Christ redeemed the benefits of the redemption that he accomplished and to conduct them to glory.

Those theological distinctions are significant and important. But from that doctrinal nexus our interest at present is in the work of the Holy Spirit in the application of redemption, and particularly in his office in the sanctification of the sinners whom Christ redeemed. In that, we bear in mind the promise of our Lord on the night on which he was betrayed, that though he was going from his disciples, "I will not," he said, "leave you comfortless; I will come to you" (John 14:18). "I will pray the Father, and he shall give you another Comforter, that he may abide with you for ever" (John 14:16). And "when he, the Spirit of truth, is come, he will guide you into all truth" (John 16:13). Christ's promise that after his resurrection he would come again to his disciples, and then to all the

---

2. Westminster Shorter Catechism, Question 6.

church that he redeemed (John 17:20), was fulfilled in that he came in the Person of his Holy Spirit who was shed forth abundantly on his church at the day of Pentecost. Now the Spirit works his work of sanctification in his people. He does that under the command of Christ (John 16:13) by communicating to them the communicable attributes of God: wisdom, holiness, goodness, and truth. That he does to the degree and to the extent that they are being prepared for the place God has ordained they should occupy in his eternal kingdom of glory.

The work of sanctification is in a special sense frequently referred to in the Scriptures as the work of the Holy Spirit. The Christian, we are told, has been "sealed with the holy Spirit of promise" (Eph. 1:13), and the Spirit has been given to the church as Joel had prophesied, "I will pour out my spirit upon all flesh" (Joel 2:28; Acts 2:16–17). As Ezekiel conveyed God's promise, "I will put my spirit within you . . ." (Ezek. 36:27); and as Christ himself indicated that a man must be born of the Spirit if he would enter the kingdom of God (John 3:5), so the Holy Spirit is in a particular sense described to us as the agent in sanctification. God has from the beginning chosen us to salvation, we are told, "through sanctification of the Spirit" (2 Thess. 2:13). The apostle Peter adds that we are "Elect according to the foreknowledge of God the Father, through sanctification of the Spirit . . ." (1 Pet. 1:2).

But Christ, the Corinthian text says, is our sanctification. He is our sanctification through the Spirit. He is our sanctification in the further sense that it is in the perfection of his completed substitutionary work that all the benefits of redemption are grounded and from which they accrue. He is our sanctification because in our identification with him in his death and in his resurrection we too have been separated definitively from the realm and dominion of sin. But it is in the sense that it is the office of the Holy Spirit to minister to us the graces of sanctification that are in Christ that Christ is our sanctification.

There is, in the Christian's life, what the Westminster Confession refers to as "a continual and irreconcileable war" so long as this life continues for the Christian. "For the flesh lusteth against the Spirit, and the Spirit against the flesh; and these are contrary the one to the other" (Gal. 5:17). But the Confession wisely observes that "although remaining corruption," meaning thereby the remains of indwelling sin in the believer, "for a time may much prevail, yet, through the continual supply of strength from the sanctifying Spirit of Christ, the regenerate part doth overcome: and so the saints grow in grace, perfecting holiness in the fear of God."[3]

THE NATURE AND NECESSITY OF SANCTIFICATION

There is much wisdom and truth in the old theological definition that whereas justification is "an *act* of God's free grace,"[4] sanctification is an on-going process, or "a *work* of God's free grace."[5] Justification is an act, something done once and for all, because it has, at a point in time in the actual life history of the person who is justified, a purely legal or forensic character and significance. Sanctification, on the other hand, considered in its progressive aspect, has to do with the process whereby the new man in Christ is made positively holy and is gradually conformed to the image of Christ. In other terms that are frequently and properly employed, in justification Christ's righteousness is *imputed* to us, while in sanctification his righteousness is *imparted* to us.

A distinction is therefore to be made between justification and sanctification in our understanding of what they mean in the total process of our redemption. But it would be a misunderstanding to imagine that either one of these phases or aspects of redemption is achievable by the Christian, or applicable to the Christian life, without the other. To the contrary, we hold to the unbreakable unity of the process of redemption. That means that those who are in fact justified will also, by an inevitable necessity born of divine decree and operation, be sanctified, and they will, by the same inevitability of grace, be glorified (Rom. 8:29–30). That is because our salvation, in all its parts, in all its phases, its design, inception, accomplishment, and results, is the work of the grace of God. It is God alone who sovereignly accomplishes it and brings it about. God is sovereign in our election to life. He is sovereign in our justification. He is sovereign in our sanctification. And he is sovereign in the final glorification of his saints.

It should be seen, further, that in the same way as there was a definitiveness about our justification, in that we were justified and accounted righteous once and for all, so there is also a definitiveness about our sanctification. The root meaning of the word sanctify has to do with setting

3. Westminster Confession of Faith, XIII, 2–3.

4. Westminster Shorter Catechism, Question 33, italics added.

5. Ibid., Question 35, italics added.

apart, a separation to a special purpose or status or use, and a dedication to a particular and specified function. God's people of old were set apart for him in a special and peculiar way. God said to Moses, for example, that the people should keep his Sabbaths because that was to be the sign "that I am the Lord that doth sanctify you" (Ex. 31:13). And the intention of the law that God gave through Moses was that the people might thereby be set apart from all the other nations who lived in the blackness and darkness of sin. In that important sense of separation, the law was to be to the nation-church of Israel a "schoolmaster" (Gal. 3:24), to keep them until, and in order that, Christ should come. For that reason the people were to recognize their status and sanctify themselves. They were called upon to set themselves apart from every thing and from every situation unworthy of the holiness of God who had established them to be his people. The command is repeated in the Scriptures, as when Joshua said to the people, "Sanctify yourselves; for tomorrow the Lord will do wonders among you" (Joshua 3:5); or when God said to Moses in the context of the Levitical law, "Sanctify yourselves therefore, and be ye holy: for I am the Lord your God . . . I am the Lord which sanctify you" (Lev. 20:7–8).

In the Christian's sanctification the same principle comes to effect in a twofold way. First, it is God that sanctifies us, sets us apart for his own use and glory and purpose; and second, we who know ourselves to be his people by his redemption and adoption are called upon to sanctify ourselves. We are to be careful to set ourselves apart from all that we know to be contrary to his holy character and inconsistent with his precepts and law. We are told that we must "through the Spirit . . . mortify the deeds of the body" (Rom. 8:13) that we might enjoy life. We are to "put off . . . the old man . . . and put on the new man, which after God is created in righteousness and true holiness" (Eph. 4:22, 24). We are to set our "affections on things above, not on things on the earth. For ye are dead, and your life is hid with Christ in God" (Col. 3:2–3).

When we speak, then, of the necessity of sanctification, that is to be seen in both an objective and a subjective sense. Objectively, as we are by nature unclean and polluted in our state of sin, it is necessary that we be made clean and our lives transformed into the likeness of Christ whom we now serve. Now that we have a new standing in Christ it is necessary that in our sanctification his righteousness should be formed in us. In that objectively necessary change of character the pollution must be progressively changed and replaced by a new intrinsic righteousness that conforms to the likeness of Christ.

The subjective necessity of sanctification has reference, not to the actual process of renewal and sanctification itself, but to the fact that the Christian needs to know for himself, within himself and subjectively, that this process is at work and is effective. He needs to know that he is being changed into the pattern of righteousness that is in Christ. He needs to know that truly, subjectively, and clearly, because he is told to "pursue," and to pursue with all diligence, "the holiness, without which no man shall see the Lord" (Heb. 12:14). Sanctification is necessary in order that we might stand before God in the last day. We are therefore to search after it. We are to work toward it. We are to use with all diligence the means of grace provided to us that we might "grow in grace, and in the knowledge of our Lord" (2 Pet. 3:18). We have, along with that directive, the guarantee and the surety that God by his Spirit will work that work within us and bring us to the end that he has ordained. For this is the very thing that he has already undertaken to do. We can be "confident of this very thing," the apostle said, "that he which hath begun a good work in you will perform it until the day of Jesus Christ" (Phil. 1:6).

THE MEANS AND RESULTS OF SANCTIFICATION

The discussion to this point of the Christian believer's progress in sanctification has intertwined two aspects that need to be separately addressed. We have spoken of both the work of the Spirit of God and the work of the individual himself. Let us ask directly, then, what part the Christian person has to play in the process of his sanctification. In doing so, we are not concerned now with what we have referred to as the definitive aspect of sanctification, wherein the new-born person in Christ is definitively set apart for God. The question now is concerned with the Christian's actual awareness and experience of the process by which he is conformed to the righteousness of Christ. We are asking whether the Christian person, now that he has been separated from his previous life-realm of sin and darkness to a new realm of life, is, or can be or should be, active in his own sanctification.

In his regeneration the sinner is passive. For regeneration is the sovereign, secret, and unsolicited act of the Spirit of God. But now that new life has been imparted and planted within the soul, the new-born person is no longer dead in sin. He is now alive. He is able to act. And he is there-fore able to work out his progress in holiness and is, decidedly, responsible for doing so. The means of sanctification are essentially twofold: first, the diligent attention to the means of grace that we have referred to in an ear-lier context; and second, the individual's mortification of sin. The means of grace, without repetition of detail, are the reading and hearing of God's word preached, faithfulness in prayer, the faithful partaking of the sacra-ments and the true understanding of the grace of the sacraments, and the benefits of the fellowship of the saints. The matter of the mortification of sin calls for further brief comment. For there will be no progress in sanctification unless there is progress in the mortification of sin.

The Psalmist has laid down the benchmark for us: "Thy word have I hid in mine heart, that I might not sin against thee" (Ps. 119:11). The word of God provides the only true source of criteria, the only secure standard for life and thought. In it we find directions for godly living and for our growth in grace. It is there we find our warnings, our chastisement, our consolations, our comfort, and our peace, as we war in Christ's strength against the world, the flesh, and the devil. It is there we find wisdom and strength as we struggle against the forces of evil without and the remain-ing elements of sin and corruption within. It is in the word that we find the directive and the encouragement, "If we live in the Spirit, let us also walk in the Spirit" (Gal. 5:25). For "they that are Christ's have crucified the flesh with the affections and lusts" (Gal. 5:24). "Let not sin therefore reign in your mortal body, that ye should obey it in the lusts thereof . . . for when ye were the servants of sin, ye were free from righteousness . . . But now being made free from sin, and become servants to God, ye have your fruit unto holiness, and the end everlasting life" (Rom. 6:12, 20, 22). It is in the word that we are directed to "mortify the deeds of the body" (Rom. 8:13), or as the apostle Paul said of himself, "I keep under my body, and bring it into subjection" (1 Cor. 9:27).

In the working out of his sanctification the Christian, who is now alive by the Spirit of God at work within him, is able to do something he was not able to do, or had any inclination to do, or saw any significant wis-dom in doing, in his old condition. Now he is able to see the importance and necessity of dealing with his own self in such a way as to make sure he is, in all aspects of his thought and behavior, in control of himself and conforming to the pattern of God for him. The new man in Christ is, by the grace of God, in control of himself. He speaks to himself. He speaks to his unruly heart and by God's grace brings it into conformity with the word of God. He speaks to his feelings and emotions. He remonstrates with himself when his thought life, his imaginations, and his contemplations are disordered and fail to conform to the thought patterns of the word of God.

The Christian knows, too, the meaning of prayer and the importance of it as a part of his conscious pursuit of sanctification. He knows something of humiliation in prayer, and the adoration of God his Father, his maker who sustains and preserves him, his Lord who saves and succors him. He knows the worship of prayer, and he knows the cry of repentance and remorse for sin, as he knows the joy and peace of reconciliation with his God. He knows the meaning of the Psalmist's prayer, "Show me thy ways, O Lord; teach me thy paths . . . for thou art the God of my salvation; on thee do I wait all the day . . . Remember not the sins of my youth, nor my transgressions; according to thy mercy remember thou me for thy goodness' sake, O Lord" (Ps. 25:4, 5, 7). He knows, now that he is the servant of Christ, that he can "come boldly unto the throne of grace . . . and find grace to help in time of need" (Heb. 4:16). He knows with a new freedom, because his heavenly Father knows the things of which he has need, that he can "in every thing by prayer and supplication with thanksgiving let [his] requests be made known unto God" (Phil. 4:6).

In the process of his sanctification the believer will know that Christ by his Spirit ministers all the graces of sanctification to his people. And in the strength of Christ the believer can say, "I also labor, striving according to his working, which worketh in me mightily" (Col. 1:29). And yet we have to ask the question that has engaged us at several points: Do we sin? Or to ask the question in more precise terms, are we continually diligent in the pursuit of the means of grace of which we have spoken? If we are honest enough to answer that question in the negative, the further question arises as to how, then, the Spirit of God accomplishes within us the work that he has undertaken to do? The answer, in a sentence, is that he does it by imposing his discipline upon our lives. The writer to the Hebrews puts it clearly, "My son, despise not thou the chastening of the Lord, nor faint when thou art rebuked of him. For whom the Lord loveth he chasteneth, and scourgeth every son whom he receiveth" (Heb. 12:5–6). God by his Holy Spirit does not leave his people to themselves. If we are not diligent in the use of the means of grace, if we sin, if we wander from his ways, he will not leave us. He will, in all the thousand ways we will begin to perceive, so chastise us that we will be brought to do his will.

The extent of sanctification is in this life incomplete. We give no hospitality to the notion that perfection of holiness is attainable in this life. There will be in this life and until the grave what we noted the Westminster Confession refer to as the "continual and irreconcilable war" against the forces of sin and evil. But while that is so, it is nevertheless true that the Christian person will at the end be perfectly fashioned after the holiness of Christ. "Beloved, now are we the sons of God, and it doth not yet appear what we shall be," the apostle John said, "but we know that, when he shall appear, we shall be like him; for we shall see him as he is" (1 John 3:2). John is not there saying that it is because we shall see Christ in that day that we shall then be made and become like him. To the contrary, John's statement is to the effect that it is because we shall by that time have been made like Christ, by the sanctifying work of the Holy Spirit in our lives, that we shall see our Lord for who he is. At that time, the result and reward of our sanctification will be our entrance into the inheritance that God prepared for his redeemed people before the foundation of the world. Then the Christian will realize his *summum bonum*, his highest good, the perfect vision of God in Christ.

At that last great day we shall see in a fullness of truth and implication what now we see though a glass darkly. "For this cause he [Christ] is the mediator of the new testament, that by means of death, for the redemption of the transgressions that were under the first testament, they which are called might receive the promise of eternal inheritance [or, that is, the inheritance that has been promised]" (Heb. 9:15). The biblical response to all we have said regarding the believer's responsibility for, and progress in, sanctification is summed up in the statement of the apostle John to which we have referred. "Every man that hath this hope in him," John says, "purifieth himself, even as he is pure" (1 John 3:3). Therefore, "Let us lay aside every weight, and the sin which doth so easily beset us, and let us run with patience the race that is set before us, looking unto Jesus the author and finisher of our faith" (Heb. 12:1–2). In that he will never leave us or forsake us. He will be with us to the end.

9

Conclusion

IN THE PRECEDING CHAPTERS we have spoken in intentionally brief terms of questions that bear on the origin, conduct, quality, and prospects of the Christian life. Evangelical Christianity, we saw, to the extent that it is biblically consistent, has benefited from the bequest of the Reformation and post-Reformation theology, as that descended, in turn, from the seventeenth-century Puritan literature in England. A corresponding literature that came from the Netherlands in the seventeenth and eighteenth centuries, from the so-called Dutch second Reformation, can be shown to have achieved similar results.

At the heart of the meaning of the Christian faith is the sovereign decree of God that led to the substitutionary life and death of his Son in this world for the redemption of sinners. The sin that made that death necessary if any were to be redeemed was, in its essence, the assumption of human autonomy against God. That assertion of autonomy came to expression on the levels of man's being, knowledge, and behavior or ethics. More particularly, it was seen that in the new-born life of the Christian believer the same sin of assumed autonomy raises its head and diverts the Christian from his new path of righteousness. "When God converts a sinner," to recall the argument from the Westminster, Savoy, and Baptist confessions, though the individual is thereby raised to a new status in Christ, the defect of sin too easily appears. While the individual is now free to obey God and his perfect law, he is also capable of the transgression of that law. He is now free to do the good, but he does also that which is evil.

The explanation of the possibility and the fact of sin in the life of the Christian is not to be found in the Christian's possession of two natures, an old sinful nature and a new regenerate nature. We noted the appearance, and at certain times the widespread influence, of such a false "theory" of the Christian character and life. The explanation of post-regenerate sin, we found, was in the fact that though the Christian is, in the sanctity of what we called his integral personhood, one new nature, there remains in him an old "principle of action." That old principle, or *habitus*, conflicts with the new principle of action that is conveyed to the soul in God's sovereign act of regeneration. To that extent, the prevalence or the dominating and action-determining influence of the old principle is being gradually diminished in the course of the believer's sanctification.

It is a not uncommon experience, we observed, that the Christian soul becomes aware of the loss of the light of the countenance of God, and the withdrawal of the conscious awareness and the heart-warming assurance of the presence of the Spirit of God. The cause of that is traceable to the presence of sin in the believer's life. That sin is to be characterized, in one way or another, as following from the same, but no doubt subtle and unnoticed, assumptions of autonomy that in a blatant way explained our first parents' fall.

The counteracting force in the life of the Christian that guards and guarantees his perseverance is his diligent attention to the demands of progress in sanctification. While God is clearly, as the Scriptural data establish, sovereign in sanctification as in justification and every other aspect of one's redemption, the believer does have an important part to play in his or her sanctification. The Christian is to "work out [his or her] salvation with fear and trembling," and to get to work to mortify the sins of the body and the lusts of the flesh. But the completion of sanctification, the final and complete conformation of the redeemed individual to the likeness of Christ, is guaranteed. God makes Christ to be the sinner's sanctification, as he is the ground of the sinner's justification, and the work that is directed to that end is carried on by the ministry to the soul of the Holy Spirit of God, the Spirit whom Christ, with the Father, has sent to be our Comforter.

As a result of all that has been said, what, then, is to be said of the obligations that devolve on the Christian believer as a result? The Christian is to live out his days in this world to the glory of God and witnessing to the truth as it has been revealed in Jesus Christ his redeemer. Monasticism and asceticism in their misguided forms, and the myriad expressions of mistaken exclusivism, find no vindication in the Scriptures that guide the Christian life. The Christian is to be "the salt of the earth" (Matt. 5:13), with all the inconspicuous efficiency with which salt does its job. But the church, while it preaches the gospel to the world and announces the good news of salvation, is also "a city that is set on a hill." The people of God have a clear task and responsibility: "Let your light so shine before men, that they may see your good works, and glorify your Father which is in heaven" (Matt. 5:16). Christianity is to be seen by the possessors of it as capable of influencing the social and cultural structures of the world. But it will be effective in doing so only as the Christian understands the obligation it carries with it, obligations that are concerned with the cultivation of a Spirit-filled life on the one hand and a biblically-determined perspective of external responsibilities on the other.

Christ is made unto us, we have seen, wisdom and righteousness and sanctification. It is with our condition of ignorance, guilt, and pollution that the grace of Christ deals, and it is against our misery, which otherwise points to eternal perdition, that he is made our redemption. If we were to look for the word, the notion, or the idea that most illustratively stands in contrast to redemption it would be that of bondage. In an all-embracing sense it is from the bondage of sin that Christ has redeemed us. It is from the dominion of the "strong man armed" (Luke 11:21) that Christ has rescued us. The sinner's life in this world is, as a result of his bondage, a miserable life. That is blazoned to us every day by the world, in its newspapers and novels, its craze for diversion, and in its communications media. There is no wholesomeness of life outside of Christ. There is no rest for the wicked. They "are like the troubled sea, when it cannot rest, whose waters cast up mire and dirt. There is no peace, saith my God, to the wicked" (Is. 57:20–21). Here we see misery, an empty meaninglessness in this life, the vanity of pretense and ragged illusion, and in the life to come eternal despair.

But when the time comes at which a man knows he is lost, when he sees his misery for what it is, then he can know that it is against this misery that Christ is his redemption. If he could have found satisfaction in himself, or if there had been any other source of relief, he would never have come to Christ. But in doing so he sees, in the solitude of his own moment of self-realization, both the misery in which he stands and his escape from it in the mercy of Christ.

Before we leave our summary of the perspectives we have established, we observe that God has laid on all men everywhere an obligation to believe the gospel that the church is commissioned to announce. "God now," Paul said to the Athenians, "commandeth all men everywhere to repent" (Acts 17:30). All are called to repent of transgressions against the law of God. We do not repeat what has been said regarding the demands of that law. But it is worthy of emphasis that the law in its moral aspect, as that is encapsulated in the Ten Commandments, is itself a rearticulation and republication of the law of righteousness as it was given to our first parents. As such it is to be understood as a creation mandate that lays its obligations on all people everywhere and at all times. That being so, the moral law not only calls the sinner to repentance, but it remains the rule of life for the Christian believer. In the moral law we see the reflection of God's holiness, the holiness which in Christ we are called upon to emulate. It is that that lies determinatively behind the call to the Christian, "Be ye holy, for I am holy" (1 Pet. 1:16; Lev. 20:7).

The moral law provides the Christian's benchmark or criteria of belief and action. It provides the Christian's moral imperatives. There can be no higher calling than to live according to it, in the strength of purpose and resolve that the grace of Christ imparts. The high calling the Christian possesses is grounded in the fact that now, by the redeeming grace of God, he is joined to Christ in a vital, spiritual, and indissoluble union.

But what we might see as a final aspect of that high calling engages us. The apostle Paul raised the issue in his letter to the Ephesian church. "Be not drunk with wine," he says, "wherein is excess." I know, he says in effect, that what I am about to refer to may well produce effects in your lives that ordinary men will not understand and that they may mistakenly confuse, as they did on the day of Pentecost, with the effects of having taken wine in excess. But I am speaking of something, a character and manner of life, which is altogether and profoundly different, he continues. And then he says in all directness and in arresting simplicity, "But be filled with the Spirit" (Eph. 5:18). That is the thing that should now arrest our spiritual consciousness, that we should be filled with the Spirit. The apostle is not speaking here of a spirit of love or joy or patience or meekness. He is not speaking of what in another place he referred to as the fruit of the Spirit. On the contrary, when he says here, "Be filled with the Spirit," he is speaking about the Holy Spirit himself.

We must be filled with the Spirit. Our lives are to be taken up by him. We must do all that is required of us that Christ by his Holy Spirit might be formed in us. We must know with a clear awareness what is unworthy of him and with resolution turn aside from all such things and allegiances and be done with them. We must be sure that we do not "grieve" him (Eph. 4:30) as we wait on him and know his developing ministry in our lives;

not waiting for him in the sense of desiring and waiting for this or that particular experience, but waiting upon him for all of the blessing that he sovereignly ministers to his people.

The Psalmist knew something of all this. "Rest in the Lord, and wait patiently for him," he says (Ps. 37:7), and Isaiah knew something of what it is we stand in need of, "They that wait upon the Lord shall renew their strength; they shall mount up with wings as eagles; they shall run, and not be weary; and they shall walk, and not faint" (Is. 40:31). We have it on the authority of our Lord himself that our "Father [will] give the Holy Spirit to them that ask him" (Luke 11–13). May God come to us by his Spirit in this impoverished day.

Bibliography

à Brakel, Wilhelmus. *The Christian's Reasonable Service*. Vol. 1. Translated by Bartel Elshout. Grand Rapids: Reformation Heritage Books, 1992.

_____. *The Christian's Reasonable Service*. Vol. 2. Translated by Bartel Elshout. Grand Rapids: Reformation Heritage Books, 1993.

Alexander, C. F. *There is a Green Hill Far Away*. In *Trinity Hymnal*. Atlanta: Great Commission Publications, 1990. Also various hymnals.

Augustine. *Confessions*. Translated by Henry Chadwick. Oxford: Oxford University Press, 1991.

Bavinck, Herman. *The Doctrine of God*. Translated by William Hendriksen. Edinburgh: Banner of Truth, 1977.

_____. *Reformed Dogmatics: Volume 2: God and Creation*. Translated by John Vriend. Grand Rapids: Baker Academic, 2004.

_____. *Reformed Dogmatics: Volume 3: Sin and Salvation*. Translated by John Vriend. Grand Rapids: Baker Academic, 2006.

Beeke, J., and Sinclair B. Ferguson. *Reformed Confessions Harmonized*. Grand Rapids: Baker Books, 1999.

Berkhof, L. *Systematic Theology*. Grand Rapids: Eerdmans, 1939.

Boston, Thomas. *Human Nature in its Fourfold State*. London: Banner of Truth, 1964.

Brown, John. *An Exposition of the Epistle of Paul the Apostle to the Galatians*. Minneapolis: Klock & Klock, 1957.

Browne, Thomas. *Hydriotaphia*. Accessed March 28, 2008. Online: http://www.uoregon.edu/~rbear/browne/hydriotaphia.html.

_____. *Religio Medici*. Accessed March 28, 2008. Online: http://www.uoregon.edu/~rbear/browne/medici.html.

Buchanan, James. *The Doctrine of Justification*. Edinburgh: Banner of Truth, 1961.

Calvin, John. *Commentaries on the Epistle of Paul the Apostle to the Romans*. Translated and edited by John Owen. Grand Rapids: Baker Book House, 1979.

_____. *Commentary on the Epistles of Paul the Apostle to the Corinthians*. Translated by John Pringle. Grand Rapids: Baker Book House, 1979.

_____. *Institutes of the Christian Religion*. Translated by Ford Lewis Battles. Edited by John T. McNeill. Philadelphia: Westminster Press, 1960.

Cherry, Conrad. *The Theology of Jonathan Edwards: A Reappraisal*. Bloomington: Indiana University Press, 1990.

Clark, Gordon H. *Thales to Dewey*. Unicoi, TN: Trinity Foundation, 1977.

_____. *What is Saving Faith?* Unicoi, TN: Trinity Foundation, 2004.

Clark, R. Scott, ed. *Covenant, Justification, and Pastoral Ministry: Essays by the Faculty of Westminster Seminary California*. Phillipsburg, PA: P&R Publishing, 2007.

Bibliography

Cowper, William. *O for a closer walk with God*. In Congregational Union of England and Wales. *Congregational Praise*. London: Independent Press, 1958. Also various hymnals.

Cunningham, William. *Historical Theology*. London: Banner of Truth, 1960.

Dabney, Robert L. "Theology of the Plymouth Brethren." In *Discussions: Evangelical and Theological*. London: Banner of Truth, 1967.

Dallimore, Arnold. *George Whitefield: The Life and Times of the Great Evangelist of the Eighteenth-Century Revival*. Edinburgh: Banner of Truth, 2 vols., 1970 and 1979.

Descartes, R. *Discourse on Method and The Meditations*. Translated by F. E. Sutcliffe. New York: Penguin, 1968,

Duncan, J. Ligon. "The Attraction of the New Perspective(s) on Paul. Accessed March 29, 2008. Online: http://www.alliancenet.org/partner/Article_Display_Page/0,,PTID307086%7CCHID560462%7CCIID1660662,00.html.

Edwards, Jonathan. *Charity and Its Fruits*. Edinburgh: Banner of Truth, 1969.

———. *The End for Which God Created the World*. In John Piper. *God's Passion for His Glory*. Wheaton: Crossway Books, 1998.

———. *Freedom of the Will*. Morgan, PA: Soli Deo Gloria Publications, 1996.

Einstein, A. *Out of My Later Years*. London: Thames and Hudson, and New York: The Philosophical Library, 1950.

Elliott, Paul M. *Christianity and Neo-Liberalism*. Unicoi, TN: Trinity Foundation, 2005.

Eveson, Philip H. *The Great Exchange: Justification by faith alone—in the light of recent thought*. Leominster, UK: Day One Publications, 1996.

Ferguson, Sinclair B. *John Owen on the Christian Life*. Edinburgh: Banner of Truth, 1987.

Flavel, John. "The Method of Grace in the Gospel Redemption." In *The Works of John Flavel*. London: Banner of Truth, 1968.

Flew, Anthony. *An Introduction to Western Philosophy: Ideas and Arguments from Plato to Popper*. London: Thames and Hudson, 1989.

Frame, John. *No Other God: A Response to Open Theism*. Phillipsburg, PA: P&R Publishing, 2001.

Gaffin, Richard B. *"By Faith, Not by Sight": Paul and the Order of Salvation*. Milton Keynes, UK: Paternoster, 2006.

———. "Paul the Theologian." *Westminster Theological Journal*, 62 (2000) 121–141.

———. *Resurrection and Redemption: A Study in Paul's Soteriology*. Phillipsburg, PA: P&R Publishing, 1978.

Geehan, E. R. *Jerusalem and Athens: Critical Discussions on the Theology and Apologetics of Cornelius Van Til*. Philadelphia: Presbyterian and Reformed, 1971.

Harnack, Adolf. *History of Dogma*. Translated by James Millar. New York: Dover, 1951.

———. *Outlines of the History of Dogma*. Translated by E. K. Mitchell. Boston: Beacon Press, 1975.

Helm, Paul. *Eternal God: A Study of God without Time*. Oxford: Clarendon Press, 1988.

Hendriksen, William. *New Testament Commentary: Exposition of Ephesians*. Grand Rapids: Baker Book House, 1979.

Henley, William Ernest. *Invictus*. Accessed March 28, 2008. Online: http://www.bartleby.com/103/7.html.

Henry, Matthew. *An Exposition of the Old and New Testament*. Vol. 9. London: James Nisbet, 1880.

Hodge, Charles. *A Commentary on 1 & 2 Corinthians*. Edinburgh: Banner of Truth, 1974.

———. *Systematic Theology*. London: Thomas Nelson, 1873.

Bibliography

Horton, Michael S. *Covenant and Salvation: Union with Christ.* Louisville: Westminster John Knox, 2007.

Howe, John. "The Living Temple." In *The Works of the Rev. John Howe.* Ligonier, PA: Soli Deo Gloria Publications, 1990.

Hughes, Philip Edgcumbe. *Paul's Second Letter to the Corinthians.* Grand Rapids: Eerdmans, 1962.

Kant, I. *Critique of Pure Reason.* Translated by J. M. Meiklejohn. Amherst, N.Y.: Prometheus, 1990.

Kuyper, Abraham. *Principles of Sacred Theology.* Grand Rapids: Eerdmans, 1963.

Lloyd-Jones, D. M. *God's Ultimate Purpose: An Exposition of Ephesians 1:1 to 23.* Grand Rapids: Baker Books, 1979.

_____. *God's Way of Reconciliation: Studies in Ephesians chapter 2.* London: Evangelical Press, 1972.

_____. *Romans: An Exposition of Chapter 6, The New Man.* London: Banner of Truth, 1972.

_____. *Romans: An Exposition of Chapters 7:1—8:4, The Law: Its Functions and Limits.* Edinburgh: Banner of Truth, 1973.

Lusk, Rich. "A Response to 'The Biblical Plan of Salvation.'" In *The Auburn Avenue Theology . . . The Knox Theological Seminary Colloquium on the Federal Vision.* Fort Lauderdale, FL: Knox Theological Seminary, 2004.

Luther, Martin. *The Bondage of the Will.* Translated by J. I. Packer and O. R. Johnston. Westwood, NJ: Fleming H. Revell, 1957.

Mackintosh, Hugh Ross. *Types of Modern Theology: Schleiermacher to Barth.* New York: Scribners, n.d.

Martin, Robert P. *Accuracy of Translation and the New International Version.* Edinburgh: Banner of Truth, 1989.

Milton, John. *Paradise Lost.* In M. H. Abrams, et al. eds. *The Norton Anthology of English Literature.* New York: Norton, 1962.

Murray, John. *Collected Writings of John Murray.* Edinburgh: Banner of Truth, 1977.

_____. *The Epistle to the Romans.* Vol. 1. Grand Rapids: Eerdmans, 1959.

_____. *Principles of Conduct.* Grand Rapids: Eerdmans, 1957.

_____. *Redemption: Accomplished and Applied.* Grand Rapids: Eerdmans, 1955.

Newton, John. *Amazing Grace.* In *Trinity Hymnal.* Atlanta: Great Commission Publications, 1990. Also various hymnals.

Nicoll, W. Robertson, ed. *The Expositor's Greek Testament.* Grand Rapids: Eerdmans, 1979.

Orthodox Presbyterian Church. *Justification: Report of the Committee to Study the Doctrine of Justification.* Willow Grove, PA: Committee on Christian Education of the Orthodox Presbyterian Church, 2007.

Owen, John. *The Death of Death in the Death of Christ.* London: Banner of Truth, 1959.

_____. *The Nature and Power of Indwelling Sin.* In *The Works of John Owen,* Vol. 6. Edinburgh: Banner of Truth, 1967.

_____. *Of the Mortification of Sin in Believers.* In *The Works of John Owen.* Vol. 6. Edinburgh: Banner of Truth, 1967.

_____. *Pneumatologia, A Discourse Concerning the Holy Spirit.* In *The Works of John Owen.* Vol. 3. Edinburgh: Banner of Truth, 1965.

Packer, J. I. "Introductory Essay." In James Buchanan. *The Doctrine of Justification.* Edinburgh: Banner of Truth, 1961.

Piper, John. *God's Passion For His Glory*. Wheaton: Crossway Books, 1998.

Poole, Matthew. *A Commentary on the Holy Bible*. London: Banner of Truth, 1963.

Presbyterian Church in America. *Report of the Ad Interim Committee on Federal Vision, New Perspective, and Auburn Avenue Theologies*. Accessed March 29, 2008. Online: http://www.pcahistory.org/pca/07-fvreport.pdf.

Reymond, Robert L. *A New Systematic Theology of the Christian Faith*. Nashville: Thomas Nelson, 1998.

Ridderbos, Herman. *Paul: An Outline of His Theology*. Edinburgh: Banner of Truth, 1973.

Robertson, O. Palmer. *The Current Justification Controversy*. Unicoi, TN: Trinity Foundation, 2003.

Sanders, E. P. *Paul and Palestinian Judaism*. Minneapolis: Fortress Press, 1977.

Savoy Declaration of Faith (1658). Millers Falls, MA: First Congregational Church, 1998. Also various editions.

Schaff, Philip. *History of the Christian Church*. Grand Rapids: Eerdmans, 1981.

Schleiermacher, Friedrich. *The Christian Faith*. Edinburgh: T & T Clark, 1928.

_____. *On Religion: Speeches to Cultured Despisers*. New York: Harper & Row, 1958.

Scofield, C. I. *Rightly Dividing the Word of Truth*. Fincastle, VA: Scripture Truth Book Company, n.d.

Scougal, Henry. *The Life of God in the Soul of Man*. Harrisonburg, VA: Sprinkle Publications, 1986.

Second London (Baptist) Confession (1689). Accessed March 28, 2008. Online: http://www.vor.org/truth/1689/1689bc00.html. Also various editions.

Shedd, W. G. T. *A History of Christian Doctrine*. New York: Charles Scribner's Sons, 1868.

Shepherd, Norman. *The Call of Grace: How the Covenant Illuminates Salvation and Evangelism*. Phillipsburg, PA: P&R Publishing, 2000.

_____. *Thirty-Four Theses on Justification in Relation to Faith, Repentance, and Good Works*. Presented to the Philadelphia Presbytery of the Orthodox Presbyterian Church, 1978. Accessed March 29, 2008. Online: http://www.hornes.org/theologia/norman-shepherd/the-34-theses.

Sproul, R. C. *The Consequences of Ideas: Understanding the Concepts That Shaped our World*. Wheaton: Crossway Books, 2000.

_____. *Faith Alone: The Evangelical Doctrine of Justification*. Grand Rapids: Baker Books, 1995.

Stendahl, Krister. "Paul Among the Jews." In *Paul Among the Jews and Other Essays*. Minneapolis: Fortress Press, 1977.

Turretin, Francis. *Institutes of Elenctic Theology*. Vol. 1. Phillipsburg, PA: P&R Publishing, 1992.

_____. *Institutes of Elenctic Theology*. Vol. 2. Phillipsburg, PA: P&R Publishing, 1994.

Van Til, Cornelius. *A Christian Theory of Knowledge*. Philadelphia: Presbyterian and Reformed, 1969.

_____. *An Introduction to Systematic Theology*. Philadelphia: Presbyterian and Reformed, for the Den Dulk Christian Foundation, 1974.

_____. *Apologetics*. Philadelphia: Westminster Theological Seminary, Class Syllabus, n.d.

_____. *Common Grace*. Philadelphia: Presbyterian and Reformed, 1954.

_____. *The Defense of the Faith*. Philadelphia: Presbyterian and Reformed, 1963.

Venema, Cornelis P. *Getting the Gospel Right*. Edinburgh: Banner of Truth, 2006.

_____. *The Gospel of Free Acceptance in Christ*. Edinburgh: Banner of Truth, 2006.

Venning, Ralph. *The Plague of Plagues*. London: Banner of Truth, 1965.

Bibliography

Vickers, Douglas. *Christian Confession and the Crackling Thorn*. Grand Rapids: Reformation Heritage Books, 2004.

_____. *Divine Redemption and the Refuge of Faith*. Grand Rapids: Reformation Heritage Books, 2005.

_____. *The Fracture of Faith: Recovering belief of the gospel in a postmodern world*. Fearn, Scotland: Christian Focus Publications, Mentor Imprint, 2000.

Vos, Geerhardus. *The Pauline Eschatology*. Grand Rapids: Eerdmans, 1961.

Waters, Guy Prentiss. *The Federal Vision and Covenant Theology*. Phillipsburg, PA: P&R Publishing, 2006.

_____. *Justification and the New Perspectives on Paul: A Review and Response*. Phillipsburg, PA: P&R Publishing, 2004.

Watts, Isaac. *Our God, Our Help in Ages Past*. In *Trinity Hymnal*. Atlanta: Great Commission Publications, 1990. Also various hymnals.

Westminster Confession of Faith (1647). In *Trinity Hymnal*. Atlanta: Great Commission Publications, 1990. Also various editions.

Westminster Larger Catechism (1647). In Johannes G. Vos. *The Westminster Larger Catechism: A* Commentary. Phillipsburg, PA: P&R Publishing, 2002. Also various editions.

Westminster Shorter Catechism (1647). In *Trinity Hymnal*. Atlanta: Great Commission Publications, 1990. Also various editions.

Wilkins, Steve. "Apostasy and the Covenant (II)." Lecture delivered at the 2001 Auburn Avenue Presbyterian Church Pastors' Conference.

_____. "The Legacy of the Half-Way Covenant." Lecture delivered at the 2002 Auburn Avenue Presbyterian Church Pastors' Conference.

Wilson, Douglas. *"Reformed" is not Enough*. Moscow, ID: Canon Press, 2002.

_____. "A Short Collection of Credos: On Baptism." *Credenda/Agenda* 15/5:24, #6. Accessed March 29, 2008. Online: http://www.credenda.org/issues/15-5credos.php.

Windelband, W. *A History of Philosophy*. New York: Macmillan, 1921.

Witsius, Herman. *The Economy of the Covenants between God and Man*. Phillipsburg, PA: P&R Publishing, for the Den Dulk Christian Foundation, 1990

Wright, N. T. *What Saint Paul Really Said: Was Paul of Tarsus the Real Founder of Christianity?* Grand Rapids: Eerdmans, 1997.

www.ingramcontent.com/pod-product-compliance
Lightning Source LLC
Chambersburg PA
CBHW060342100426
42812CB00003B/1092